T0323590

Cambridge Elements ≡

Elements in Contemporary Performance Texts
edited by
Fintan Walsh
Birkbeck, University of London
Duška Radosavljević
Royal Central School of Speech and Drama, University of London
Caridad Svich
Rutgers University

COMEDY AND CONTROVERSY

Scripting Public Speech

Sarah Balkin
The University of Melbourne
Marc Mierowsky
The University of Melbourne

CAMBRIDGE
UNIVERSITY PRESS

Shaftesbury Road, Cambridge CB2 8EA, United Kingdom

One Liberty Plaza, 20th Floor, New York, NY 10006, USA

477 Williamstown Road, Port Melbourne, VIC 3207, Australia

314–321, 3rd Floor, Plot 3, Splendor Forum, Jasola District Centre,
New Delhi – 110025, India

103 Penang Road, #05–06/07, Visioncrest Commercial, Singapore 238467

Cambridge University Press is part of Cambridge University Press & Assessment,
a department of the University of Cambridge.

We share the University's mission to contribute to society through the pursuit of
education, learning and research at the highest international levels of excellence.

www.cambridge.org
Information on this title: www.cambridge.org/9781009565356

DOI: 10.1017/9781009396820

First published 2024

A catalogue record for this publication is available from the British Library

ISBN 978-1-009-56535-6 Hardback
ISBN 978-1-009-39680-6 Paperback
ISSN 2753-2798 (online)
ISSN 2753-278X (print)

Comedy and Controversy

Scripting Public Speech

Elements in Contemporary Performance Texts

DOI: 10.1017/9781009396820
First published online: December 2024

Sarah Balkin
The University of Melbourne

Marc Mierowsky
The University of Melbourne

Author for correspondence: Sarah Balkin, sarah.balkin@unimelb.edu.au

Abstract: This is an Element about stand-up comedy and public speech. It focuses on the controversies generated when the distinction between the two breaks down, when stand-up enters – or is pushed – into the public sphere and is interpreted according to the scripts that govern popular political and media rhetoric rather than the traditional generic conventions of comic performance. These controversies raise a larger set of questions about the comedian's public role. They draw attention to the intention of jokes and their effects in the world. And they force us to consider how the limits of comic performance – what can be said, by whom, and why – respond to, and can reshape, public discourse across changing media contexts.

Keywords: comedy, stand-up, comic persona, free speech, controversy, social media

ISBNs: 9781009565356 (HB), 9781009396806 (PB), 9781009396820 (OC)
ISSNs: 2753-2798 (online), 2753-278X (print)

Contents

1 Introduction: Comic Performance and Public Speech

This Element is about stand-up comedy and public speech. It focuses on the controversies generated when the distinction between the two breaks down, when stand-up enters – or is pushed – into the public sphere and is interpreted according to the scripts that govern popular political and media rhetoric rather than the traditional generic conventions of comic performance. These controversies raise a larger set of questions about the comedian's public role. They draw attention to the intention of jokes and their effects in the world. And they force us to consider how the limits of comic performance – what can be said, by whom, and why – respond to, and can reshape, public discourse across changing media contexts.

The relation of comic performance to society at large has been the focus of serious stand-ups since the 1950s and 1960s. Our focus is different in that each of the controversies covered here was driven by social media and fuelled by expanded digital distribution and reception contexts. Streaming and social media have made comedy available to wider and more diverse audiences than ever before, but often at the expense of removing the comic performance from the context that distinguishes it from other kinds of speech and rhetoric. Stewart Lee observed this decontextualising process at its inception (or close to it) and warned against the effects it would have on the performance, reception, and analysis of stand-up. These effects are discernible in the controversy surrounding his 2009 special *If You Prefer a Milder Comedian, Please Ask for One,* during which Lee told a joke about Richard Hammond, presenter of the wildly popular *Top Gear.* Referring to Hammond's near fatal crash in a jet-powered dragster and the memoir he published after it, Lee riffs on the idea that Hammond has 'been able to carve out a best-selling literary career off the back of his own inability to drive safely'. Irked by the apparent cynicism of Hammond's profiteering, he takes a characteristic slide into the absurd: 'I wouldn't be surprised if when he was hanging upside down waiting to be rescued, he wasn't thinking to himself, "ooh, I hope I get some brain damage and forget loads of my life. And then on Richard and Judy's Book Club my attractive wife can come on and help me to remember it and it'll create a tender scene"'. After making a claim that the British public should be the ones cashing in on the crash – after all, it was a BBC show and their licence fees that paid for it – he comes to the part of the joke that was to generate serious public backlash:

> I think it's a cynical thing to do, and I hate him for it, and I wish he'd been killed in that crash. Well, I do. I wished he'd been killed and … and decapitated, and that the next series of *Top Gear* had been presented by

Jeremy Clarkson, James May and Richard Hammond's severed head on a stick. [*Walks to the front of the stage.*] And if that seems a bit much for all the *Top Gear* viewers . . . .it's just a joke, like on *Top Gear*. You know, when they do their jokes, which you like, don't you?—the Jeremy Clarkson defence —'It's just a joke'. So when I said that I wished Richard Hammond had been decapitated and kicked, right, like when they do their jokes on *Top Gear*, it was just a joke. But coincidentally . . . as well as it being a joke, it's also what I wish had happened. (Lee 2012: 57–60) [italic in the original]

The *Daily Mail* picked up the bit and, shearing it from its context, spun it into a story of deep-seated animosity, looking for reasons why Lee, who went to the same school as Hammond (though their paths did not cross, a fact Lee turns into a joke as part of the show), would harbour such murderous hatred (Tapper 2009). Other tabloids followed suit, and internet message boards became a forum for what Lee calls the '"toxic mess" of *Top Gear* loyalists and *Daily Mail* readers', most of whom had not seen the show and yet still felt able to express 'the desire that I be banned, though from what was not always clear' (2012: 67).

Lee has been called the comedian's comedian, in part for his refusal to embrace the widely appealing and unchallenging model he associates with Michael McIntyre 'spoon-feeding you [the audience] his warm diarrhoea' (2012: 29), and in part for routines that incorporate a continual meta-analysis of his art and practice. We could just as easily call him the comedy scholar's comedian for these deeply self-reflexive shows and the books he publishes in their wake, in which he extends his analysis from comic form and technique to the reception of particular jokes, audience management, the experiments in form and content he undertakes, how he alters a joke from performance to performance, what spurs these variations and how they change the nature of the routine and allow his comedy to evolve (Lee 2011, 2012). Perhaps it's safer not to, given how he skewered poor Alan Bennett when the writer attempted to account for how Lee renders stand-up 'almost a moral pursuit' by terming him 'the J.L. Austin of what is now rather a sloppy profession' (Bennett 2019). As is his practice, Lee read the review on stage, stoking audience derision by lampooning the incongruity of Bennett's linguistic and philosophical frame of reference when the object of his critique was a ratty alternative comedy show (Lee 2022c). We should note that, while Lee makes fun of Bennett's highfalutin manner, he never denies the upshot of Bennett's comparison: that jokes do things in the world.

Had the outraged readers of the *Daily Mail* seen *If You Prefer a Milder Comedian* or waited to read the book (of the same title) that analyses the performance, they would have realised that their reaction proves Lee's point.

As he explains, referring to another joke directed at the *Top Gear* presenters, 'I make the indefensible joke, and attempt to defend it using glib *Top Gear* logic, to show that the *Top Gear* logic, in and of itself, is not enough' (2012: 64). By saying 'it's only a joke' Lee exposes the hollowness of the presenters and their viewers who license all manner of racist, sexist, classist, and homophobic comments as 'jokes', accusing all who object of being humourless and kowtowing to political correctness. Lee's attacks against *Top Gear*, its morally compromised presenters, and the viewers they target – '[a] kind of frightened middle-aged man in his house, he's scared of how the world's changing, and political correctness has gone mad, and he likes to watch *Top Gear,* don't you? "Cause it pays . . . it pays no heed to the political correctness or the women's rights or the gays' rights"' (2012: 55) – anticipates present-day debates on wokeness, cancel culture, and the limits of comic speech. But the controversy the joke generated also positions it on the cusp of changes within the media ecosystem that are arguably more significant for the practice and analysis of stand-up comedy today: these changes have unsettled the (never truly stable) relationship between comic performance and public speech.

Lee was acutely aware of such developments. *If You Prefer a Milder Comedian* came on the back of season one of his successful TV show *Stewart Lee's Comedy Vehicle* (2009–16). This once cult figure of alternative comedy was now more widely known. With Lee's combative and often difficult stage persona, any embrace by the mainstream threatens his outsider status, changing his relationship to his audience and the standpoint from which he critiques society. As Matt Hargrave (2020: 73) notes, Lee 'has increasingly had to reinvent his marginalisation because of his commercial success'. As comedians become more recognisable, their gigs, as Lee points out, risk becoming 'less like a comedy show and more like a prolonged personal appearance' (2012: 7). Audiences are less likely to receive what they say according to the generic expectations of the stand-up stage and liable to understand comic words and actions by the less permissive expectations placed on other kinds of public figures. Accompanying this flattening out of generic difference, Lee noted, '[m]ore irritatingly, there was now Twitter, and portable internet technology, to monitor one's every move' (2012: 11–12). Though Lee recognised the potential for social media as a way for comics to get work (2011: 40), the fact that people were tweeting his jokes did not simply mean they were taken out of context,[1] but that they were publicised to such

---

[1] A problem that has faced comedians from the outset of stand-up comedy (see our section on persona, pg. 27, where a policeman repeats Lenny Bruce's routine in front of the grand jury).

a degree that he could no longer follow the tried and true path of experimenting with sets in small clubs, honing and refining them before bigger audiences. For Lee, looking back on his first show under this changed environment, he felt forced to ask: 'does public mass exposure to stand-up prime people to understand the genre implicitly and to accept greater experimentation with form and content, or does it programme them to accept, in fact, a narrower field of options, the idea of what stand-up can be becoming ossified in the process?' (2012: 99).

#justjokes

Since Lee first posed this question the changes to social and digital media have only accelerated. During this period, 'it's only a joke' has become shorthand for stereotypically right-wing defenders of comedy against stereotypically humourless left-wing 'snowflakes'.[2] A good example of how these discourses and media converge is Australian comedian Hannah Gadsby's presentation of the award for direction in a drama series at the 2018 Emmy Awards. The appearance followed Gadsby's international breakout comedy special *Nanette*, which called out straight white men and criticised comedy for its misogyny and homophobia on the cusp of the #MeToo movement against sexual harassment and assault. Many of Gadsby's critics, including comedians such as Norm Macdonald and Emmy co-host Michael Che, noted in interviews and on social media that Gadsby was not funny, that *Nanette* was not comedy, or that they were tired of 'anti-comedy comedy' (Sobel 2018, Wright 2018).[3] 'What are jokes these days?' Gadsby asked on stage at the Emmys in the aftermath of this public controversy. 'We don't know. Nobody knows what jokes are, but especially not men. Isn't that right, fellas?' (Bradley 2018). Noting the ridiculousness of somebody like them, 'a nobody from nowhere', presenting at the Emmys, Gadsby added, 'Free suit, new boots. Just because I don't like men! That's a joke, of course. Just jokes, fellas, calm down. Hashtag Not All Men. But a lot of them!' (Bradley 2018). Like Lee, Gadsby turns the 'just jokes' defence, which would conventionally be aimed at feminist or otherwise left-wing objectors, on men in order to show its inadequacies. The hashtag that conventionally accompanied posts during the #MeToo movement here becomes spoken discourse marking Gadsby's live comment as part of a social media conversation. *Vanity Fair* followed Gadsby's lead when the magazine headlined its reporting on this moment, 'Did Hannah Gadsby Just Subtweet Her Nastiest Critics at the

---

[2] See Nesteroff 2023: 14, 16 on how these sorts of culture war narratives have been spread by think tank media operatives.

[3] Macdonald and Che also both insisted they had not seen *Nanette*, though it was the clearest example of what Che called 'anti-comedy comedy' circulating at the time.

Emmys?' (Bradley 2018). A subtweet is a Twitter post that refers to a particular user without explicitly mentioning them.[4] The implication, made explicit in the subheading, is that Gadsby did the live equivalent of subtweeting Che at the Emmys broadcast.[5]

To return to Lee's question, then, social media scripts do prime people, including comedians, to understand comedy in ways that can make the genre both more expansive and more ossified. On the one hand, our exposure to comedians is both wider and more diffuse. Our expanded media environment enables conversation across live, mediatised, and digitised performance contexts in ways that also extend the make-up of the audience. The intersections of this expanded media environment with social media discourses like #MeToo support experiments such as Gadsby's *Nanette*, which challenged the generic expectations of the performance and suggested different ways for comedians to be public figures. At the same time, as Gadsby's Emmys presentation demonstrates, contemporary expanded media environments can also contribute to informal policing of what is and is not comedy by comedians and audiences alike. The effects of all these changes and the implications they have for both the performance and serious study of stand-up comedy are the focus of this Element. Our aim is to provide some new methods to understand how comedy scripts and is scripted by contemporary public discourse. The case studies or controversies we have chosen centre on comedians from the UK, Australia, and the US. While there are differences in stand-up across these countries, they have long-standing traditions of comedians touring and, now, streaming their shows in ways that create and benefit from overlapping reception and media contexts, including transnational humour scandals. The United States' centrality in the history of stand-up and its dominance in the contemporary production and distribution of comedy in global Anglophone media through platforms such as Netflix, Amazon, and YouTube have weighted our choice of examples. Our hope is that the methods outlined nonetheless prove useful to the study of comedy beyond these cultural and geographic confines. These new methods are in many ways well established, insofar as they comprise performance and discourse analysis and attention to audience and context. What have changed are some of the media and performance contexts we analyse and the public

---

[4] Elon Musk rebranded Twitter as X in July 2023, following his acquisition of the platform in October 2022. Musk's content moderation policies make X a qualitatively different platform; as such, we refer to it as Twitter before July 2023 and X after that date.

[5] The subheading reads, 'Plenty of men have offered opinions about *Nanette,* and whether it "counts" as stand-up comedy – particularly Emmys co-host Michael Che' (Bradley 2018).

discourses that influence how comedians and audiences understand their mutual contract. Our 'new' methods, then, are about recognising patterns in how these performances, discourses, and media contexts combine and finding ways of working across them. What we propose is not a dramatic departure from existing modes of analysing comedy; indeed, our approach to contemporary stand-up is grounded in two foundational aspects of the genre: persona, the comedian's performed self, and licence, the comedian's contract with the audience. Further, our sense of what needs updating in approaches to contemporary comedy is embedded in our backgrounds as historians of comic form. Section 2 provides a long view (in short form) of how comic persona developed to better illustrate how contemporary digitised distribution and social media discourses complicate the relationship between comic performance and public speech, which we discuss in Section 3. We build especially on scholarship by Oliver Double (2014) on persona, Rebecca Krefting (2014) on 'charged humour', Dustin Bradley Goltz (2017) on comedy and internet outrage, and our own work on persona and licence.

Although comedians and comedy fans tend to idealise live stand-up, most contemporary audiences encounter comedians in recorded versions of live shows and appearances: as the hosts of comedy news, televised award ceremonies, or talk shows; via streaming specials; and in social media posts. These genres and media affect how comedians' speech is received. Stand-up is rhetorical, meaning that it operates by persuading an audience to accept the performer's worldview (Greenbaum 1999: 33). It is also public if we take 'public' to mean 'open to the scrutiny of anyone' (Sennett 1974: 16). Humour is central to twenty-first-century public discourse, which proliferates across a fragmented plurality of global, digitally networked publics (Kuipers and Zijp 2024: 5). Comedians are public figures, a category that encompasses people who hold a government office, those who have achieved celebrity or notoriety, and public intellectuals. Most comedians do not hold a government office, but the most successful ones are celebrities. As P. David Marshall (2014: xi, xxiv) discusses, building on Henry Jenkins' account of 'the participatory and convergent new media culture', celebrities 'inhabit a social space closer to us than ever before'.[6] Comedians' participation in this culture means they speak to their audiences in new ways, through new media. There is also a long tradition of viewing stand-up comedians as public intellectuals (Kofsky 1974, Jones 2009, Dagnes 2012, Aarons and Mierowsky 2017a). Edward

---

[6] On celebrity see also M. Luckhurst. (2019). Hannah Gadsby: Celebrity Stand-up, Trauma, and the Meta-Theatrics of Persona Construction. *Persona Studies*, 2, 53–66; S. Marcus. (2020). *The Drama of Celebrity*. Princeton: Princeton University Press; J. R. Roach. (2007). *It*. Ann Arbor: University of Michigan Press.

Said's (1993) definition that a public intellectual is someone 'endowed with a faculty for representing, embodying, articulating a message, a view, an attitude, philosophy or opinion to, as well as for, a public, in public' can be applied to a range of comedians. But to conflate comedians' speech with that of other kinds of public figures who profess a cohesive, sincere, discernible worldview is to ignore crucial elements of how comedy is scripted and performed. For while comic speech is political, performed comedy also differs from political rhetoric. As Goltz argues, in a contemporary 'cultural climate where comedy is so often at the centre of controversy, too often we engage comedic work as if it were parallel to political speech' (2017: 6). This lack of distinction further embroils comedians in public controversy because it complicates the conventional comedian/audience contract through which licence is established and according to which comedy performances are typically analysed.

Performance studies, which routinely attends to what performers do as well as what they say, and which considers onstage, offstage, and mediatised performances, is well placed to mitigate this tendency.[7] Both comedy and many kinds of political speech involve spoken and embodied modes of meaning-making such as facial expression, gesture, and tone of voice, and both can be analysed as performances. But they are different genres of performance, with historically different conventions of persuasion and reception. At the same time, the proliferation of comedy news and other genres of infotainment across media platforms has, for some viewers, made such distinctions less clear. Moreover, when comedians engage with the public on social media platforms, they become textual and mediatised performers whose embodiment may or may not be present as images or recordings, and whose speech may be received on different terms. The remainder of this section examines a comedian, Hasan Minhaj, who

---

[7] There is a substantial body of scholarship on live and mediatised performance. The emblematic interlocutors in this debate are Peggy Phelan and Philip Auslander. Phelan (1993: 46) argues that 'Performance's only life is in the present. Performance cannot be saved, recorded, documented, or otherwise participate in the circulation of representation of representations'. She sees these qualities as making performance independent from mass reproduction, and therefore resistant to the labour of the reproduction of capitalism. Auslander (2008: 7) rejects Phelan's premise, arguing that if live events are becoming more and more like mediatised ones, liveness cannot 'function as a site of cultural and ideological resistance'. Building on Jean Baudrillard, Auslander (2008: 4) defines mediatised performance as 'performance that is circulated on television, as audio or video recordings, and in other forms based in technologies of reproduction'. It also includes modes of live performance that incorporate media such as video. Thus, a live performance may also be mediatised in multiple ways. Our emphasis is on performances that circulate both within and outside the framework of the live 'room' of stand-up comedy, and how some of these new contexts for circulation change what comedians do and how their speech is received. For a good survey of performance scholarship on liveness and multimedia performance see S. Kim. (2017). Liveness: Performance of Ideology and Technology in the Changing Media Environment. *Oxford Research Encyclopedia of Literature*, Oxford: Oxford University Press. https://doi.org/10.1093/acrefore/9780190201098.013.76.

developed his 'sincere' persona across several live and digital platforms and who, in 2023, found his stand-up subject to fact-checking by *The New Yorker*. Our analysis of Minhaj's persona shows how comedians' proliferation across media-tised performance contexts complicates their contract with the audience. Comedy scholarship, we argue, can respond to the changed contexts in which stand-up circulates by answering three basic questions: what is the comedian's persona, how does that persona establish the comedian's licence to speak, and how do (mediatised) performance contexts shape and complicate the audience's contract with the comedian?

Fact-Checking Hasan Minhaj

In September 2023, *The New Yorker* staff writer Clare Malone fact-checked American comedian Hasan Minhaj's stand-up specials in an article titled 'Hasan Minhaj's "Emotional Truths"'. She found that several of the anecdotes related in Minhaj's comedy, which is known for its political commentary from the perspective of an Indian American man, were partially untrue. Malone accused Minhaj of changing the details of stories from his stand-up specials: for example, in his Netflix special *Homecoming King* (2017) he tells a story about being rejected by his prom date due to her family's racism. Malone (2023a) noted that Minhaj had changed the timing of the rejection when he told the story on stage and claimed that the woman who rejected Minhaj 'said that she and her family had faced online threats and doxing for years because Minhaj had insufficiently disguised her identity'. Minhaj's fans were disap-pointed that a comedian committed to highlighting oppression would lie and media responses questioned (as Malone did) his responsibilities to the real people represented in his stand-up stories (Pahwa 2023). In late September, comedy news program the *Daily Show*, which was rumoured to be considering Minhaj as its next host, announced that it would return to a guest host format for its 2024 season; media outlets and viewers assumed the controversy had cost Minhaj the prestigious gig (Walsh 2023). Minhaj (2023) then released a twenty-one-minute video on his YouTube channel, 'My Response to the New Yorker Article', subtitled 'I brought receipts', detailing the information he had provided to Malone during and after their interview and how she had used it selectively. Many X users noted Minhaj's video, which contains no jokes, changed their minds about the controversy; they subsequently charac-terised Malone's article as a 'hit piece' by a white woman targeting a performer of colour.[8] In a review of Minhaj's December 2023 show at the

---

[8] See Malone's post (2023b) stating that she stands by her story in *The New Yorker*. As of December 2023, there were over 4,000 replies. They include, for example, Kaivan Shroff's

Beacon Theatre in Manhattan, *The New York Times* comedy critic Jason Zinoman, who had questioned whether Minhaj 'crossed a line' (2023a) in the aftermath of Malone's *The New Yorker* piece, now mused, 'this scandal might be the best thing that ever happened to him' (2023b). The Minhaj controversy is an excellent example of how contemporary public discourse and media contexts create misunderstanding about persona and licence.

As we will note more than once when discussing comic controversies, fictionalising some aspects of a stand-up performance is a conventional and well-accepted practice. It nonetheless raises questions about a comedian's contract with their audience. These questions are rooted in a tension inherent in comic persona since the mid twentieth century: although, on the one hand, it is normal to make some things up, on the other hand, 'almost every aspect of the stand-up performance has evolved to give the impression of truthfulness' (Shouse 2020: 33). Another way of thinking about this tension is to say that although most contemporary stand-up is autobiographical, it is not traditionally subject to what Phillipe Lejeune (1995: 5, 13) famously called the 'autobiographical pact' – the idea that if the author's name on the cover is the same as that of the narrator and the main character, then readers should be able to assume identity between the three. In contrast, as we discuss in Section 2, in stand-up, the traditional presumption is that the speaking persona is a version of the performer, but that performed self may be heightened or diverge in various ways from the factual details of the comedian's life. But in our contemporary context, several aspects of comedy, not least its distribution across genres and media platforms, have led audiences and comedians alike to question comedians' responsibilities to be truthful, and what truthfulness means.[9]

Both Malone and Minhaj frame the question of his truthfulness as a problem of persona. Minhaj's persona was established across two genres: comedy news and stand-up. His breakout role as a correspondent on the *Daily Show* from 2014–18 aligned him with comedy news, a televised genre associated with comedians John Stewart, Stephen Colbert, John Oliver, Samantha Bee, and

---

(2023) comment, 'How can you stand by this? Do you dispute any of this?' with a link to Minhaj's response video. For another representative reply, see Sid Dani (2023): '@ClareMalone You ruined a man's career and his chance to host the Daily Show. Do you realize that? Your audacity to say, "We stand by our story", is appalling. You wrote a hit piece. Journalists like you are causing the public to lose trust and faith in mainstream media'.

[9] For example, anxiety about being called to account for fictionalising in his foray into print authorship appears to have led Minhaj's fellow *Daily Show* alum Aasif Mandvi to issue a 'disclaimer' on the copyright page of his book, *No Land's Man*: 'Although the stories in this book are based on true events, the specific circumstances are often a blend of fact and imagination. Some of the names, identifying characteristics, and circumstances have been changed ... sometimes for the better, but that's just my opinion' (2015).

Trevor Noah. Minhaj's Emmy-winning Netflix show *Patriot Act* (2018–20), the title of which references the post-9/11 statute that expanded what qualified as terrorism and gave US law enforcement increased scope for surveillance, was likewise a weekly comedy news program that aimed to 'explore the modern cultural and political landscape "with depth and sincerity"' (de Moraes 2018). Comedy news programs report real events in a satirical manner, with the hosts often supported by a team of fact-checkers. This basis in fact makes comedy news feel journalistic even as it is parodic, with comedy news hosts often sent out to cover real stories such as American presidential elections.[10] Although comedy news hosts often emphasise that what they do is not journalism, studies have shown that during the early 2000s many young adults got their news from these shows (McBeth and Clemons 2011: 80). Further, a range of politicians including candidates for the American presidency have appeared on comedy news shows to announce their runs, lending a sense of political legitimacy and efficacy to the genre that comedians nonetheless call 'fake news'.[11] Scholarship on comedy news (Baym 2005: 262, McBeth and Clemons 2011: 92) argues convincingly that the perceived blurring of 'fake' and 'real' news responds not only to comedy news shows' basis in fact, but also to the 'real' or traditional news' failure to contribute to an authentic critical discourse and democracy (2011: 92).

While comedy news shows satirise traditional news media, news networks also 'regularly replay political comedy segments, and in the fall of 2009 CNN fact-checked a *Saturday Night Live* (SNL) sketch about President Obama – promptly getting skewered by the *Daily Show* … for doing so' (McBeth and Clemons 2011: 79). While the *Daily Show*'s skewering attempted to hold up an

---

[10] Minhaj has experienced the convergence of different kinds of public speech as a comedy news host. For example, following an episode of *Patriot Act* that criticised Saudi Arabia for the killing of *Washington Post* columnist Jamal Khashoggi ordered by the country's crown prince, Netflix was asked to remove the episode from its platform in Saudi Arabia. A Saudi regulator cited a law prohibiting the 'production, preparation, transmission, or storage of material impinging on public order, religious values, public morals, and privacy, through the information network or computers' (Stewart 2019). Netflix complied but Minhaj still received death threats on Twitter, some of which he displayed on slides in his stand-up special *The King's Jester* (2022). Minhaj acknowledged to Malone (2023a) that these were not authentic but were 'heightened for comedic effect'. In the stand-up special, Minhaj describes the social media death threats as the first time he had 'clout', noting that subsequently *Time* magazine nominated him one of the *Time* 100 most influential people in the world. During sequences about the fame and clout he attracted due to this and other social media eruptions, Minhaj adopts a somewhat demonic voice and facial expression to denote its corrupting influence on him. On the implications of Netflix's compliance with Saudi Arabia's request for global digital media, see Khalil and Zayani 2021. See also Elkins 2021.

[11] A good example of the blurred line between 'real' and 'fake' news on comedy news shows was when US Senator John Edwards became the first candidate to announce he was running for president on *The Daily Show* in 2003. Stewart joked that Edwards might need to re-announce elsewhere because the show was 'fake' (O'Neil 2003).

important distinction between comedy and journalism, the phenomenon of fact-checking political comedy is indicative of the perceived blurring of genres and their accompanying ethical imperatives. Indeed, in a 2019 interview, Minhaj and *The New Yorker* staff writer Vinson Cunningham frame *Patriot Act* as moving beyond the *Daily Show*'s mantra that it is 'just comedy'. Cunningham notes Minhaj's 'earnestness' and 'seriousness of intent' and Minhaj comments that not only do many people get their news from shows like *Patriot Act*, but these shows have also been known to break news, as when Minhaj broke the story that a US military document issued to soldiers on training missions in Saudi Arabia contained outdated and racist language; as a result of this story, the United States Central Command (CENTCOM) issued a formal apology and removed the document from its website (Husband 2018). Shane Herron (2022: 184) notes that in the years since *The Colbert Report* broadcast its final episode in 2014, comedy news shows 'are often little more than news or current affairs programs with the occasional comic flourish thrown in for color'. But while the CENTCOM story is an example of a comedian breaking news, Minhaj (Minhaj and Cunningham 2019) maintains there are still different conditions for speech in play: 'for my job the necessary condition is comedy; the sufficient condition is is this news, is this interesting', whereas for journalists, 'the necessary condition is news; the sufficient condition is is it interesting', with the added critique that for 'cable news and a lot of certain sort of click baiting media the necessary condition is is it salacious'. This is the cultural and media climate in which Malone (2023a) declared that 'in informing the public', comedians 'assume a certain status as moral arbiters'.

But it was Minhaj's stand-up specials that Malone fact-checked. In the article, she notes, 'When it came to his stage shows, he told me, "the emotional truth is first. The factual truth is secondary"' (2023a). In his response video Minhaj plays an expanded excerpt of this moment in their recorded interview, accompanied by a visual transcript, where he distinguishes his personae at greater length:

> HASAN. When people see a 'Hasan Minhaj' show, there's two different expectations, there's the 'Hasan Minhaj' you see, maybe here at the Comedy Cellar, where there is an implicit agreement between the audience like we're going down into a basement, like we're about to see a one-hour comedy show that feels like there is an emotional roller-coaster ride . . .

> REPORTER. Sure.

> HASAN. Then there's 'Hasan Minhaj', the guy you've seen on The Daily Show as a correspondent or the guy from Patriot Act on Netflix, which is I am not the primary character. The news story is the primary character . . .

> . . . with the latter, the truth comes first. Comedy sometimes comes second to
> make the infotainment, the sugar on the medicine. In this [stand up comedy],
> the emotional truth is first, the factual truth is secondary. (Minhaj 2023,
> ellipses and brackets in original.)

It is true that comedy news and stand-up are different genres with different
audience expectations attached to them. But, as Malone (2023a) points out,
Minhaj's distinction between his stand-up and comedy news personae
'seemed to sidestep the possibility that most people likely don't parse which
Hasan Minhaj they're watching at a given moment'. Minhaj is right that
audiences who see a show at New York's Comedy Cellar are likely to be
fans of stand-up comedy and therefore familiar with its conventions. But by
grounding his implicit agreement with the audience in the act of going down
into a basement to see a live show, Minhaj repeats a fallacy we have heard
from other contemporary comedians (discussed in Section 3) whose expanded
audiences are on Netflix or other digital platforms. What is the implicit
agreement between Minhaj and audiences who watch both *Patriot Act* and
his stand-up specials on Netflix or YouTube?[12] This is not to say that Netflix
and YouTube audiences cannot tell the difference between stand-up and
comedy news, but they may not perceive Minhaj's persona as the point of
differentiation.

Indeed, although Minhaj's stand-up is grounded in first-person storytelling in
a way that comedy news is not, both personae are notable for their sincerity.
Minhaj establishes this sincerity through a mix of tone, expression, and visual
cues. In *The King's Jester* (2022), for instance, although Minhaj tells many
jokes, he also tells moralising stories about himself and others. In this show
Minhaj performs a bit about 'Brother Eric', an FBI informant who was attempting to entrap Muslim youth when Minhaj was a teenager. Minhaj details a scene
in which, having pretended to Brother Eric that he planned to get his pilot's
licence, the police suddenly swarmed Minhaj's local gym and slammed him
against the hood of car. This is one of the stories Malone (2023a) fact-checked;
Minhaj admitted to her that it was not based in literal truth, but that as a teenager
he and other Muslim friends did play basketball with middle-aged men who the
boys suspected were officers. In the special, Minhaj also displays slides of
newspaper headlines that show the kind of story he tells about Brother Eric did
happen to real people: for example, a real headline (Rybarczyk 2004) from the
Chicago Tribune reads, 'ACLU says FBI spied on activists, Muslims'. As
Minhaj tells stories about young people such as Hamid Hayat, whose conviction

---

[12] The team behind *Patriot Act* made all episodes available on YouTube (Khorana 2022: 53),
demonstrating their recognition of these viewers as a core part of Minhaj's audience.

for supporting terrorism was overturned after Hayat had served fourteen years of his sentence (Flynn 2019), he repeatedly points accusingly at the audience and down at the stage.[13] 'Man, he's my age, he's thirty-six', Minhaj says with anger in his voice. 'I think about Hamid all the time'. Minhaj explains that this story is why he called his comedy news show *Patriot Act*. 'It was my middle finger to Brother Eric, you understand?' As he announces this, the camera, which for much of this story has filmed him at an angle from a distance, shifts to a straight-on close-up of Minhaj's serious face. Behind him on a slide is the logo for *Patriot Act*. The live audience, who have been silent for most of Minhaj's story, burst into applause, a phenomenon known as 'clapter comedy' – when the purpose of a joke is to make the audience applaud and agree rather than laugh.

The Brother Eric bit is 'emotional truth' in the sense that stories *like* the one Minhaj told really happened, and his naming of *Patriot Act* was doubtless a response to a period that negatively impacted Muslim Americans.[14] One might say that the story is true to the genre rather than the letter of Minhaj's lived experience as a second-generation immigrant who grew up during this post-9/11 period. It might also be considered appropriate for a performer from a heavily surveilled community to deliberately distort some information – indeed, Malone implicitly accuses Minhaj of not distorting enough by failing to protect his prom date's identity, highlighting that there are ethical and unethical reasons to change the details of a story. But our aim is not to judge whether Minhaj did wrong by changing the details of his story: as we have noted, it is conventional for comedians to fictionalise. If the Brother Eric story strikes a sour note, for us this is because of the moralising tone in which Minhaj tells it rather than because of the fictionalising as such. More interesting is the way Minhaj's Brother Eric story is also an origin story for *Patriot Act*, bringing his personae closer together. Indeed, many of the stories in *The King's Jester* involve Minhaj narrating the personal or professional consequences of bits he performed on *Patriot Act*. Minhaj's practice of using PowerPoint slides that shore up his performance's truth claims with seemingly factual evidence, which is consistent across his comedy news, stand-up, and

---

[13] In the special, Minhaj inaccurately says Hayat served twenty years of his sentence.

[14] As Bilici (2010: 196–97) notes, the 'negative charisma' associated with being Muslim during this post-9/11 period of increased surveillance and racism also opened the field for Muslim comedy in the United States. For example, the comedy troupe Allah Made Me Funny (Bryant 'Preacher' Moss, Azhar Usman, Azeem Muhammad, Mohammed 'Mo' Amer) was founded in 2003, with the troupe Axis of Evil (Ahmed Ahmed, Maz Jobrani, Aron Kader, Dean Obeidallah) following in 2005. Minhaj, a practicing Muslim, emphasises a generational South Asian American racialised experience as well as religious identity in his comedy (see Michael 2018: 63, Pennington 2024: 90).

YouTube video rebuttal of *The New Yorker* article, likewise makes it difficult to separate his personae. Sometimes this evidence *is* factual, as when he shows real newspaper headlines. At other times, as we discuss presently, the visuals are fictionalisations. Does it matter? In Malone's (2023a) article, Minhaj admitted to changing some details 'in service to a bigger point'. Zinoman (2023a) notes that while 'embellishing in the name of a larger truth is what comics do', Minhaj's 'style, onstage and often off in interviews, suggested we should believe him'. For Lejeune (1995: 13–14), the paratextual elements of an autobiography, especially the title page, are key to its pact with the reader. For Minhaj and other comedians who use comedy news-style PowerPoint slides, visual supports that may conventionally be understood as paratextual, or interviews that might conventionally be understood as paratheatrical, are often part of the extended performance – sometimes of a particular show, but more broadly of a persona that exceeds the bounds of a particular genre or performance context. It is not surprising, with these mediatised perform-ance practices in play, that the contract between performer and audience is unclear.

Perhaps ironically, then, *The King's Jester* (2022) ends with an appeal to the audience's ability to distinguish between satire and sincerity. As part of the setup for this appeal, Minhaj details a story about what kinds of comic speech are legally protected. He narrates a Netflix attorney's response to Minhaj's idea of putting up a series of billboards around the United States declaring vulture capitalist 'Randall Smith loves pedophiles'. Though the billboards are fictional, in *The King's Jester* they are illustrated in all caps on slides behind Minhaj alongside maps marking their prospective locations in American cities where Smith's company is taking over local news organisa-tions. The stunt, which Minhaj did not carry out, raises the question of what kinds of comic speech are legally protected. Minhaj says that the Netflix attorney begged him not to go through with the billboard idea because it is defamation that breaches the 'reasonable person standard' in US tort law, which states that 'a joke is clearly not defamation if it's clearly a joke to a reasonable person'. Minhaj notes that a world full of reasonable people is the kind of world he wants to live in. He projects this hope onto his audience, adding, 'I want to be able to switch between satire and sincerity and trust that you know the difference. Trust that you won't take me out of context. Everything here tonight is built on trust; why do you think I'm performing in this LED skate park?' Minhaj's shift to joking midway through the last sentence references the set and his practice as a self-proclaimed (2022) 'PowerPoint' comedian. His use of supporting slides and clips across *Patriot Act* and his stand-up specials deploys the visual language of comedy news, which itself parodies the visual language of network news. In this sequence in *The King's Jester*, then, Minhaj models how he shifts between sincerity and satire, teaching the audience how to read the 'fake news' aspects of the stand-up set in context. At the same time, he acknowledges that his sincere persona is built on premeditated performance choices that involve but extend beyond the performer's embodiment. Minhaj acknowledges as well that the two-way trust he ascribes to the audience is a rhetorical hope rather than an actuality when he quips, 'You trust me, I trust you ... that's why I locked up your phones'.[15]

Lionel Trilling defines sincerity as 'a congruence between avowal and actual feeling' (1972: 2). Sincerity involves being true to oneself 'for the purpose of avoiding falsehood to others'; thus, the moral purpose of sincerity is in the service of 'the correct fulfilment of a public role' (1972: 9). It is 'surely no accident', he adds, 'that the idea of sincerity, of the own self and the difficulty of knowing and showing it, should have arisen to vex men's minds in the epoch that saw the sudden efflorescence of the theatre', the early modern period (1972: 10). In the twentieth century, Trilling argues, sincerity was supplanted by authenticity, which involves 'a more exigent conception of the self and what being true to it consists in ... and a less acceptant and genial view of the social circumstances of life' (1972: 11). Like sincerity, authenticity involves being true to oneself, but the authentic self is a demanding one that may not strive to fulfil a social role. Interestingly, it is authenticity rather than sincerity that is most often invoked in discussions of stand-up and comic personae. For instance, Gadsby (2022: 234) describes how as they became a more confident performer, their self-deprecating persona began to feel less authentic, and 'authenticity is the secret sauce of successful comedy'. The audience, who expected Gadsby to maintain the persona with which they were familiar (2022: 234), became a barrier to what Gadsby understands as an authentic persona – a performed self that is true to their actual self. Minhaj's sincere persona is different, and perhaps less authentic, in Trilling's terms. When Minhaj and others refer to his persona as sincere, they mean something more particular to his subject matter and style of delivery. This comes through in a podcast interview between journalist and media analyst Brooke Gladstone and comedy critic Jesse David Fox: what Minhaj is 'great at', Gladstone

---

[15] Gadsby acculturated comedy audiences to the practice of securing their phones in locked pouches during the performance on their tour of *Douglas* (2019, 2020 on Netflix). Gadsby's stated reason is that they are autistic and find the distraction of audience phone use distressing, but other comedians have applauded and implemented the practice to prevent audience members recording and distributing clips from their shows on social media (Smith and Keane 2019).

(2023) notes, 'is sincerity'. Fox agrees: 'What he can do that may be better than any other comedian ever is look directly into a camera and say something earnest, I think is maybe a better word, without irony, truly just directly being like, "This is something that happened. This is important"' (Gladstone 2023). But Gladstone and Fox agree that 'earnest righteous discussion is in fact his brand'. Thus, while as a sincerely political comedian Minhaj aims to fulfil a public role, Minhaj's brand also fits Trilling's diagnosis of what happened to sincerity during the twentieth century: 'we play the role of being ourselves, we sincerely act the part of the sincere person, with the result that a judgement may be passed upon our sincerity that it is not authentic' (Trilling 1972: 11). Importantly, this does not mean that Minhaj does not actually hold the political beliefs he professes as a comedian. But it brings into relief the tensions inherent in the performance of a sincere comic persona and related questions about who the audience is, and what public role Minhaj fulfils for them.

In consultation with the Netflix attorney, Minhaj found a legal way to make his joke about Randall Smith: in *The King's Jester* he shows a slide from *Patriot Act* of himself in front of another slide of Randall Smith (represented by a drawing of 1980s alien E.T.) and American financier and sex offender Jeffrey Epstein along with a large pink heart with 'Randall Smith ♥ Pedophiles' written on it. Overlaying it is text in all caps that reads, 'THAT IS NOT TRUE'. The attorney approves the bit, but the following week Minhaj receives a letter from Smith's own legal team 'regarding your "comedy" show Patriot Act and the false accusations it makes about Mr. Smith'. The letter calls for 'a retraction of the defamatory falsehoods'. In *The King's Jester* Minhaj (2022) shows the letter on a slide and jokes that he is not offended by being sued, but is offended by the fact that 'comedy' appears in quotation marks. Minhaj then shows a slide of his own legal team's response, which reads, 'Any defamation claim brought by Mr. Smith would fail as a matter of law. Allow me to explain the jurisprudence of jokes'. The letter goes on to note, 'The second flaw in your letter is your inability to understand context. Mr. Minhaj delivers all his jokes with eyes bugging and arms flailing. As you know, many people have said Mr. Minhaj looks like a raccoon on Adderall'. During this sequence, the camera shifts between its conventional position facing Minhaj to another position between the performer and the slides projected behind him. This allows the camera to capture Minhaj as he turns around to read from the slide, with the live audience behind him. The text from the letter appears floating beside Minhaj, excerpted in large type, until he turns around to face the audience again when he gets to the racoon part. Just before he says 'raccoon on Adderall' he pauses and then gets louder, seemingly inviting the audience to say it with him, acknowledging over-animation and hyperactivity as part of his persona. The slide behind Minhaj then highlights a third part of the letter: 'As you know in New Times Inc v. Isaacks, the Supreme Court of Texas said the audience is "no dullard", and that, He or she can tell the difference between satire and sincerity'. 'You know when I'm joking. You know when I'm being serious', Minhaj verbally reinforces in the special.

Comedians have not always felt so comfortable with the legal protections afforded by persona and context, as our discussion of Lenny Bruce in Section 2 shows. Our contemporary context brings different challenges. Who is the 'you' that knows when Minhaj is joking? It presumably encompasses his Netflix audience as well as his live one. Both the live and Netflix versions of *The King's Jester* are mediatised in ways that appear to shore up the show's truth claims or, at other times, its parody of the visual language of such claims. Whether these visual cues are factual or fictionalised (it would be a misnomer to describe the slides as 'sincere') is less easy to parse, as when Minhaj shows a slide with a 'heightened' (Malone 2023a) version of the tweeted death threats he received following his criticism of Saudi Arabia on *Patriot Act*. Indeed, we increasingly felt that such claims spiralled down a rabbit hole, as in the moments when Minhaj appears in *The King's Jester* in front of PowerPoint slides of himself appearing in front of PowerPoint slides on *Patriot Act*. The visual cues of Minhaj's set and PowerPoint slides often work in tension with his 'bugged-out eyes' and 'raccoon-on-Adderall' animation. That is, although it is clear to the audience when he is joking, and although joking and seriousness are compatible aspects of comedy, the basis of Minhaj's jokes seems to be (but is not always strictly) factual. His sincerity is part of his performed persona, which is not to say it is a lie.

Minhaj's work offers a clear instance of the need for new approaches to comedy that are at once multi-modal and comprehensive of all the ways comic meaning is made. Stand-up's imbrication with the real-world events and genres of public speech that are fodder for its political commentary is long-standing. But as performed and political 'events' become more mediatised and virtual – without therefore becoming less real in their existence and effects – we should re-examine comedians' foundational beliefs about their contracts with their audiences. In so doing we can better articulate how comic controversies are scripted by and provide insight into contemporary public speech.

2 Persona

The comedian on stage is not the same as the comedian off it. This might seem a truism, but the distinction between persona and performer, in both its maintenance and breach, has to be understood if we are to grasp the complex relation between performed comedy and public discourse. Long considered a hallmark of modern stand-up, the adoption of the comic persona is rarely straightforward. Because it involves a continual negotiation between the identity of the performer and how they perform that identity, the space between persona and performer remains the source of some of stand-up's most heated public controversies.

Histories of comedy tend to identify the first formal flickers of modern stand-up in the vaudeville halls of late nineteenth-century America (Double 2014: 23–26), where performers mixed monologues with songs, card tricks, and soft shoe shuffles. As vaudeville lost currency in the 1930s, elements of the comic monologue carried through other performance spaces, albeit split along ethnic lines. For Jewish comedians, there was the Borscht Belt: the string of resorts and holiday camps in the Catskills in upstate New York where Henny Youngman, Buddy Hackett, and Mel Brooks got their starts. Borscht Belt fare was typically made up of one-liners, heavily reliant on a set-up punch-line format, and told by what Gerald Nachman calls 'efficient but anonymous joke merchants' (2003: 22).[16] For Black comedians, there was the Chitlin' Circuit: the network of theatres across the East Coast, South, and upper Midwest where comedians performed with jazz bands and singers and in front of largely Black audiences. Chitlin' Circuit comedians like Moms Mabley (stage name for Loretta Mary Aiken) and Rudy Ray Moore (who performed as Dolemite, the pimp) blended character work with sketches and stand-up, creating more distance between themselves and their on-stage characters than is typically found in present-day stand-up.

One aspect that characterised the work of comedians who broke out of these ethnic enclaves and into the comic mainstream like Dick Gregory (who got his start on the Chitlin' Circuit) and Lenny Bruce (who emerged from the tradition of the Borscht Belt) was the construction and adoption of a highly individualised stage identity (Oppliger and Shouse 2020). These stage identities were usually based on biographical experience and public markers of character but embellished and adapted to humorous effect (Aarons and Mierowsky 2025). In

---

[16] The term 'stand-up' occurs earlier (Double 2017). But the particular modern style, defined by the adoption of a persona based on the experience and identity of the comedian emerges in the mid twentieth century (Aarons and Mierowsky 2014).

performing as versions of themselves, Gregory and Bruce were at the vanguard of a widespread shift towards a more authentic, truthful, and personal style of comedy (Oppliger and Shouse 2020: 12). As noted in the introduction, Eric Shouse argues that in the wake of this shift 'almost every aspect of the stand-up performance has evolved to give the impression of truthfulness' (2020: 33). While this shift to a personal style was pervasive, it was not uniform. Balkin notes how some comedians have interpreted this genre convention 'as something like an ethical imperative' to present an authentic self, while others distance their stage identity from their sense of personhood (2023: 152).

Oliver Double classes the development of these stage identities in all their varieties under the term 'Personality'. For Double, one of the fundamental features of stand-up is that it 'puts a person on display in front of an audience, whether that person is an exaggerated comic character or a version of the performer's own self' (2014: 19). We have opted to use the term persona instead. In the first place, persona emphasises the art and technique involved in establishing and maintaining one's stage personality. In the second, it signals how this identity is serialised across a performer's career. It is through serialisation that a comedian's persona becomes the basis for their interaction with multiple audiences, the vantage point of their observational style, the source of their world view – and, in many cases, the standard against which the consistency of this worldview is judged.

We begin this section by tracing some earlier precedents for this kind of serialised persona. Setting the development of the comic persona within a more expansive literary-historical and performance context allows us to examine precisely how the persona in modern stand-up offers comedians both a distinct world view and the necessary distance from self and society to provide both insight and licence. We then question how social media has altered this crucial aspect of stand-up, as comedians engage new audiences in ways that collapse the distinction between persona and performer. Taking the careers of Sarah Silverman and Dave Chappelle, and their clashes over gender, race, and antisemitism as our primary case study for understanding how new media form and deform the comic persona, we issue a provocation: has comic persona become so closely tied to identity that it limits what comedy as a genre can usefully discuss?

The Comic Persona: A Potted History

One of the earliest attempts in English to distinguish between a 'person' and a 'persona' comes in Thomas Hobbes's *Leviathan* (1651). According to Hobbes's definition, 'a person is the same thing that an actor is, both on the stage and in common conversation, and to personate is to act, or represent himself or another' (Hobbes 1996: 112). For Hobbes, personation was one means by which representative authority was enacted: a persona allowed for, and was constituted by, speaking for another person or group of people. There's an imperfect analogy between the composite persona of Hobbes' political thought and contemporary newsbooks, in which groups of writers assumed a single, serialised public persona (Neavitt 2012). As Joanna Piccioto argues, titles like *Mercurius Melancholius* – at once the newspaper and the collective persona of its writers – 'were imaginatively understood as iterations of persons into which other people could enter': writers and readers, alike, were formed by their entrance into the disposition or political stance that governed the newsbook's identity (2022: 322).

In the early decades of the eighteenth century, the pseudonymous identities adopted by writers of periodicals like Joseph Addison and Richard Steele in *The Spectator* did not completely veil their authors. The freedoms these writers took in content and form were thus less a function of anonymity than of how these public personae were crafted and perceived. Aaron Hill's preface to the collected periodical *Plain Dealer* (1730) canvasses how the public personae of early English essayists licensed the liberties of personal divulgence and the free, associative style that marked the essay form. In Hill's words:

> The Spectator, and Nestor Ironside, are characters also excellently well adapted to our Pleasures by our Knowledge of their being Fictitious: For such is our Malignity of Temper, that we can't forgive a real Author acting or thinking oddly or idly, though our Entertainment arises from thence, because we consider him as a reasonable Man, and obliged by a superior Duty to another kind of Behaviour. (1730: 1–33)

Mr Spectator was Joseph Addison and Richard Steele's shared persona in *The Spectator* (1711–12) and Nestor Ironside was Steele's pseudonym in *The Guardian* (1713). They worked, in Hill's assessment, to give the writers room to stray, to examine themselves and their thoughts as each figure traced his meandering way through the world. According to Scott Black, the accepted fiction of these personae allowed the diversions and divagations of the essay form that English readers like Aaron Hill found too rudely personal and structurally unmoored when communicated directly from author to reader, as in the work of the French originator of the form Michel de Montaigne (2020: 139).

The personae adopted in eighteenth-century periodicals prefigure the deployment of personae by stand-up comedians in three crucial ways. (1) They allow for a distinct first-person perspective; (2) they allow distance from the author that gives licence to examine self and society; and (3) they facilitate a formal freedom allowing diversion and digression. Such freedoms of form and content were negotiated through serialisation. Across the run of the periodicals, Addison, Steele, and their contemporaries honed their personae to the point where they existed in the public sphere as fully formed identities with their own outlooks and views, related to but separable from their authors. These personae became vehicles to draw readers into debate (with the personae themselves and with other readers). In doing so, they activated and mediated the engagement of a critical public that they helped bring into being. In Habermas' account of the emergence of the bourgeois public sphere, this honing of critical capacities in the literary realm was a vital training ground. Readers who exercised their critical skills in journals and periodicals brought these skills to bear on the political public sphere, where questions of state and governance were the object of critique (Habermas 1989: 31–36, 49–50). Though the historicity of Habermas' account has drawn much criticism (Fraser 1990, Downie 2005, Kuipers and Zijp 2024), the eighteenth century remains pivotal to theorisations of the public sphere, cited as the period when private individuals came together to discuss topics of wide concern (Sennett 1974), a practice that constituted a place that was distinct from the state – a place where public opinion was formed and arbitrated. In Michael Warner's formulation, public discourse is 'poetic' in that it is both 'self-organising' and self-creating: it creates the public it seeks to address by addressing it. For Warner, the conditions that allowed this mode of discourse to flourish emerged in the West between the late sixteenth and late eighteenth centuries (Warner 2002: 113–14, 64). When set against the composite personae of the eighteenth-century periodicals and the theoretical accounts elaborated on the period they scripted, the personae of modern comedy are suddenly both historically deeper and more deeply implicated in creating the conditions for what we think of as public speech than first assumed.

Developments in nineteenth-century performance on both sides of the Atlantic further contributed to the emergence of comic persona. English actor Charles Mathews (1776–1835) popularised a form of solo entertainment known as the 'At Home', 'blending anecdotes, reminiscence, narrative, imitations and comic songs' (Davis 2015: 196). With this genre of solo performance Mathews did not develop one persona, but many personages; he was often praised for transforming instantly into these characters (Davis 2015: 199). But because he performed imitations rather than exaggerated mimicry, Mathews' style was seen as respectable even as he portrayed vulgar characters (Davis 2015: 196, 202). In this way the performer disappeared into and yet was seen as distinct from his comic personae. One of Mathews' imitations, the Yankee Jonathan, was picked up by American actor James H Hackett, contributing to an emergent landscape of American humour that Constance Rourke characterises as dominated by three main types: the Yankee, the backwoodsman, and the blackface minstrel (Rourke 1931). These types, with their distinct regional, dialectical and racialised characterisations, could be performed by any number of comedians. Because comedians often specialised in a particular type, their shared specialisation contributed to what was in essence a composite persona. Across the nineteenth and early twentieth centuries, these composite personae and stock types formed a major part of the variety and vaudeville repertoires.

One of these types, the Yankee, gave rise to a more individuated predecessor to the modern stand-up persona in the nineteenth-century American platform comedian Artemus Ward (Charles Farrar Browne). Ward first became famous writing comic sketches in the character of a touring Yankee showman. His writing, which circulated widely in newspapers and was collected in humour books, was full of intentional misspellings and a comic Yankee dialect. He was Abraham Lincoln's favourite humourist and Mark Twain's biggest influence. In late 1861, Ward tried his hand at comic lecturing. But although he retained the same name as his textual showman persona, as a touring lecturer Ward did not speak in Yankee dialect. Instead, his performance style was characterised by gravity and digression: he earnestly delivered a lecture, 'The Babes in the Wood', that never got around to its stated subject. In Ward's comic lectures, we see one of the most direct predecessors to the deadpan personae that appear on the vaudeville stage and that proliferate in modern and contemporary stand-up.[17]

In contrast to Ward's understated white Yankee showman persona, minstrelsy's stock roles and nostalgic depictions of plantation slavery helped proliferate stereotypes about excessively 'lively', over-emotional ethnic subjects (Ngai 2005: 93, Balkin 2020a: 53). blackface minstrelsy was by far the most popular and influential comic genre of the nineteenth century and its character conventions both persisted and shifted over time.[18] From the 1870s

---

[17] On Ward see S. Balkin. (2020). Deadpan and Comedy Theory. *A Cultural History of Comedy in the Age of Empire*. Edited by M. Kaiser. London: Bloomsbury, 43–66; S. Balkin. (2021). Transporting Humour: Artemus Ward and American Comedy in Britain. *Touring Performance and Global Exchange 1850–1960: Making Tracks*. Edited by G. Bush-Bailey and K. Flaherty. London: Routledge, 208–17; E. M. Branch. (1978). 'The Babes in the Wood: Artemus Ward's 'Double Health' to Mark Twain. *PMLA*, 5, 955–72; J. A. Greenhill. (2012). *Playing It Straight: Art and Humor in the Gilded Age*. Berkeley: University of California Press.

[18] Examples of minstrel types include Bones and Tambo, the low-comedy 'endmen' of the minstrel show; the interlocutor, the high-talking master of ceremonies; the slave character Jim Crow; the dandy character Zip Coon; and the cross-dressed 'wench'. There is a large body of scholarship on minstrelsy. Some good starting points include R. C. Toll. (1977). *Blacking Up: The Minstrel Show in Nineteenth Century America*. London: Oxford University Press; B. McNamara, J.V. Hatch, and A. Bean, editors. (1996). *Inside the Minstrel Mask: Readings in Nineteenth-Century Blackface Minstrelsy*. Hanover: Wesleyan University Press; E. Lott. (1993). *Love & Theft:*

onward there were increasing numbers of Black minstrel performers, for whom these roles presented both constraint and opportunity. Although Black minstrels performed grotesque stereotypes from the minstrel repertoire, they also gained access to new kinds of creative work, attracted public attention with their perceived authenticity, and in some cases performed for predominantly Black audiences, for whom their performances signified differently (Jones 2021: 132).[19] Another racialised type was the yellowface 'John Chinaman', a laundryman character who spoke nonsense words and excelled at imitating white behaviour; Josephine Lee (2022b: 59) thus frames the type as both a racial other and an assimilative threat.[20] Irish, Italian, Dutch (German), and Jewish types were also popular and carried their own stereotyped conventions – the drunk, belligerent Irishman; the happy, promiscuous Italian; the lazy, conservative Dutchman; and the canny but weak Jew (Mintz 1996: 20–21).[21] Iterations of these ethnic and racialised types were ubiquitous in burlesque and vaudeville, where they were seen by audiences that often included new immigrants and, in the 1920s, by Black audiences on the T.O.B.A. circuit.[22]

The early twentieth century saw increased opportunities for immigrants and performers of colour to play into as well as against ethnic and racialised types. A good example is Bert Williams, a Black vaudeville comedian who performed in blackface while casting doubt on its basis in mimeticism with his signature song, 'Nobody'.[23] Another is Lee Tung Foo, the first Chinese American

---

Blackface Minstrelsy and the American Working Class. New York: Oxford University Press; S. Johnson. (2012). *Burnt Cork: Traditions and Legacies of Blackface Minstrelsy*. Amherst: University of Massachusetts Press; D. A Jones. (2014). *The Captive Stage: Performance and the Proslavery Imagination of the Antebellum North*. Ann Arbor: University of Michigan Press.

[19] Much of the scholarship on Black minstrelsy focuses on Bert Williams, who we discuss briefly below. See also T. Fletcher. (1984). *100 Years of the Negro in Show Business*. New York: Da Capo Press; M. R. Scott. (2023). *T.O.B.A. Time: Black Vaudeville and the Theater Owners' Booking Association in Jazz-Age America* (Urbana: University of Illinois Press).

[20] See also chapter 1 of S. Metzger. (2014). *Chinese Looks: Fashion, Performance, Race* and E. K. Lee. (2022). *Made-up Asians: Yellowface during the Exclusion Era*. Ann Arbor: University of Michigan Press, 46–52.

[21] On ethnic and racialised types in vaudeville see also R. M. Lewis. (2007). *From Traveling Show to Vaudeville: Theatrical Spectacle in America, 1830–1910*. Baltimore: Johns Hopkins University Press; N. George-Graves. (2000). *The Royalty of Negro Vaudeville: The Whitman Sisters and the Negotiation of Race, Gender and Class in African American Theater, 1900–1940*. New York: St. Martin's Press; R. DesRochers. (2014). *The New Humor in the Progressive Era: Americanization and the Vaudeville Comedian*. Basingstoke: Palgrave Macmillan.

[22] Most vaudeville theatres were segregated, with Black patrons occupying the balcony or gallery. The Theater Owners Booking Association sought Black audiences and enabled Black performers to get more consistent bookings. See M. R. Scott. (2023). *T.O.B.A. Time: Black Vaudeville and the Theater Owners' Booking Association in Jazz-Age America*. Urbana: University of Illinois Press.

[23] There is a substantial body of scholarship on Williams. See for example S. Balkin. (2020). 'Deadpan and Comedy Theory' in M. Kaiser (ed.), *A Cultural History of Comedy in the Age of Empire* (London: Bloomsbury), pp. 43–66; A. Charters, (1970). *Nobody: The Story of Bert*

vaudevillian, who blended yellowface conventions with 'practices that commonly were believed to be beyond the ability of a person of Chinese descent – singing operatic and popular songs, doing ethnic impersonations, and exchanging comedic patter' (Moon 2005: 25). Borscht belt comedians like Henny Youngman and Chitlin' Circuit stars like Moms Mabley likewise played to a type, but embodied the ethnicities whose stereotypes they performed. For Jewish and Black performers, resorting to stereotype offered a form of safety as well as opportunities to own or shift perceptions of such depictions. With Youngman and Mabley performing on TV (read: to the white Protestant mainstream), exaggerating aspects of their inflection, syntax and, in Mabley's case, appearance in line with popular perceptions of their race and ethnicity allowed them to appear non-threatening. The hen-pecked Jewish husband and the toothless bedraggled woman in a house coat gave their comedy the cover it needed. These stereotypes were not the sum of Youngman or Mabley's acts. Though they made themselves the butts of their own jokes, their routines had wider social targets, including the systemic disadvantages each faced. If we set their work against the proliferation of types in nineteenth-century comedy, we see the beginnings of a shift in the relation of audience to persona. As comic personae are drawn more closely from the lived experiences of their performers, the audience gradually moves from laughing at comedians to laughing with them.

The biggest change came with the activist comedians of the 1950s and 1960s, whose stage identities directly reflected their own lives. Comedians like Mort Sahl, Dick Gregory, and Lenny Bruce did not attempt to soften the threat of their humour but pursued comic licence in order to speak truth to power. Sahl cast himself as a satirist, finding kinship with his Jewish background only insofar as it afforded him an outsider status and tradition of disputation: 'If the role of the Jew is to rock the boat and to be inquisitive – intellectually curious, that is – fine. Classic role' (Dauber 2017: 68). Sahl got his start at the Hungry-i, the San-Francisco comedy club where Dick Gregory, a Chicago native, had his set filmed for his first television appearance in 1961. Like Sahl, Gregory was a satirist more than a joke teller. For him, comedy had the potential to raise consciousness. He reflected on his own experience of being Black in America in order to point out the country's hypocrisies, and to give white society a better sense of Black America's pain. In one routine he opens with a joke: 'Now don't

Williams, Macmillan; L. O. Chude-Sokei. (2006). The Last 'Darky' Bert Williams, Black-on-Black Minstrelsy, and the African Diaspora (Durham: Duke University Press); D. Jones, 'The Black Below': Minstrelsy, Satire, and the Threat of Vernacularity, *Theatre Journal* 73 (2021), pp. 129–46; T. Post, Williams, Walker, and Shine: Blackbody Blackface, or the Importance of Being Surface, *TDR: The Drama Review* 59 (2015), pp. 83–100.

get me wrong, I wouldn't mind paying my income tax if I knew it was going to a friendly country. [*Audience laughs.*]' Gregory does not couch his intelligence in the guise of a non-threatening because disempowered stereotype. He speaks as a version of himself, eliciting laughter to relieve the tension inherent in his damning indictment of white power and how it is exercised:

> And we have a lot of racial prejudice up North, but we're so clever with it. Take my hometown, Chicago ... I mean just can't see it. When Negroes in Chicago move into one large area and it looks like we might control the votes they don't say anything to us, they have a slum clearance.
> [*Audience laughs and claps.*]
> You do the same thing on the West coast but you call it freeways.
> [*Audience laughs.*] (ABC Close Up Preport – Walk in My Shoes [1961])

The audience in the room and watching on TV were racially mixed. As Gregory moves from 'us' (Black Chicagoans) to 'they' (the generalised white power-brokers) to 'you' (the West coast white people in the room), he assumes the role of representative. The texture of his own experience gives him the ability speak for his community authentically. The brilliance of his satire gives him form and licence to convey the pain and depredations of that experience to both a white-dominated society and to audience members complicit in maintaining its domination. While he used laughter to relieve tension, Gregory was able to let the tension sit so that uncomfortable truths were allowed to reverberate – a technique Dave Chappelle has also mastered (Balkin 2023: 150). As Gregory put in during some of his Hungry-i gigs, 'If I've said anything to upset you, maybe it's what I'm here for. Lenny Bruce shakes up the puritans; Mort Sahl, the conservatives; and me—almost everybody!' (Foxx and Miller 1977: 180–81; Haggins 2007: 19).

Bambi Haggins observes how Gregory, who dressed in a Brooks brothers suit and tie whenever he appeared on stage, 'replicated in his appearance the visual construction of the legion of civil rights volunteers from SNCC (the Student Nonviolent Coordinating Committee) and CORE (Congress of Racial Equality) seen on the nightly news in the early sixties'. His 'persona exuded sophistication and provided a Black cultural position that was unapologetically urban and urbane' (Haggins 2007: 15). The fact that he combined onstage critiques of white supremacy with civil rights work (eventually leaving comedy for the movement) shows that his persona was, in Malcolm Frierson's words, 'more than a shtick'; it emerged from a sophisticated and fully realised political stance and served as a tool for cultural protest (Frierson 2020: 47).

Like Gregory's, Bruce's persona was self-consciously constructed to serve political ends. Bruce's pursuit was free speech and he was not attached to a political movement *per se*. Bruce came to his Jewish culture as an adult and incorporated Yiddish words as well as the syntax, inflections, and mannerisms of Yiddish speakers into his rapid-fire act, blending it with an urbanity and improvisational style taken from jazz. He called the practice *shpritzing* (Yiddish: spraying). Bruce sprayed the audience with jokes, harangues, and lectures, often lurching from topic to topic, following chains of association to their hyperbolic ends. *Shpritzing* allowed him to gather his routines into a loose coherence, one that centred on his persona as satirist, as the holy fool, the prophet-artist tearing down society's pieties and hypocrisies. For Bruce, being Jewish was essential to his satiric point of view as well as his sense of allegiance. Unlike Sahl, he performed his Jewishness to reinforce this position, stressing that Jewishness was something felt, not necessarily a set of religious practices. Crafting his stage persona as irrepressibly Jewish allowed him to position himself as a pariah, as part of an historically oppressed group but one whose members were experiencing upward mobility. In this way, Jewishness offered solidarity with the oppressed as well as a unique vantage on the oppressors. Bruce captures this duality in one routine, where he disputes the dictionary definition of 'Jew' as a descendent of the tribe of Judea: '*I know what a Jew is* – One who killed Our Lord'. The ironic invocation of 'our' brings to mind a mainstream from which Bruce is excluded. As he continues, this exclusion – the basis for centuries of oppression – is shown as the source of his insight. After raising and refuting the accusation that Jews are too quick to pass responsibility off on Romans, he plays with the idea that Jews might have killed Jesus, and with good reason:

> Or maybe it would shock some people, some people who are involved with the dogma, to say that we killed him at his own request, because he knew that people would exploit him. In his name they would do all sorts of bust-out things, and bust out people. In Christ's name they would exploit the flag, the Bible, and— *whew* Boy, the things they've done in his name! [italic in the original]

> This routine always goes good in Minnesota, with about two Jews in the audience. (Cohen 1987: 54–55)

Bruce turns one of the root causes of antisemitism on its head, exposing in the process the uncomfortable truth that Christianity in general and American Christianity, in particular, have been used as justifications for a slew of crimes, historical and current. His final line points to the serialised nature of stand-up: differently composed audiences are differently receptive to these truths, as they are to his reclamation of the Jew as Christ killer, the trope that allows him to embody the role of pariah, from which vantage he could expose these truths in the first place.

Multi-modal Personae and the Limits of Comic Licence

Bruce made a name for himself by challenging what could be said on stage – a championing of free speech that led to three arrests for obscenity. Though his comedy was freewheeling, his pursuit of licence was built through a careful negotiation between the persona he embodied and the audiences who came to see him. Bruce typically played in small clubs. The audiences he attracted knew his reputation and were conditioned by it to expect shows that challenged and even attacked them. These self-selecting audiences came knowing Bruce would 'vent his outrage' upon them, as a *The New York Times* article from May 1959 described his performances (Cohen 1987: 268; Aarons and Mierowsky 2017b: 159). As Bruce saw it, problems with his act only arose when the bond between persona and audience was broken. This was the reason for his arrests, or so he claimed on stage:

> I figured out after four years why I got arrested so many times ... see what happened, it's been a comedy of errors. Here's how it happened: I do my act at perhaps 11 o'clock at night, little do I know that at 11 am the next morning before the grand jury somewhere is another guy doing my act who's introduced as Lenny Bruce in substance.
> [*Audience laughs faintly.*]
>
> Here is Lenny Bruce in substance. A police officer who is trained for to recognise clear and present dangers not make-believe does the act. The grand jury watches him work and they go 'that stinks'.
> [*Audience laughs.*]
>
> But I get busted and the irony is I have to go to court and defend *his* act.
> (MrAndocalrisian 2010) [italic in the original]

Bruce introduces the bit with the well-worn dictum that 'you can say fire in a crowded theatre, so long as you're on stage', adding 'the theatre is make-believe, that's where it's at'. The point he makes is that there are certain performance conditions that allow greater licence than would be permitted in everyday speech. One of these conditions is that by attending the set, the audience consents to enter into a compact with the comedian. They consent to the act and can revoke consent by withholding laughter, heckling, or leaving. A second condition is the audience's awareness of his persona. The police officer cannot be Lenny Bruce 'in substance' because for Lenny Bruce, personal style is essential to that substance: it is his unique style and the persona he has crafted across multiple performances that makes his act good (the 'act' performed before the grand jury 'stinks'). The upshot is that it is his style and reputation as Lenny Bruce that help cultivate the 'make-believe': the set of conditions that he believes separate his performance from the social and legal norms governing speech.

(Comedy has its own norms for governing speech, as we discuss in Section 3.) When removed from a mutually consensual performance context and divorced from his persona, the conditions for comic licence dissolve.

Sarah Silverman, the comedian working today who best embraces Bruce's model (Aarons & Mierowsky 2017b), makes a similar point in a 2019 interview with the *Los Angeles Times*. Discussing the polarisation of political discourse and the resulting inability of the public to appreciate ambiguity, irony, and nuance, she gives the following example:

> And that's why, when you see transcripts of, like, a comic's joke, or two different people who said the same thing—in one case it could be OK and in one case it could be … up. Why? Because the intent matters, and what the person's soul is. My whole first special is in character, and I say, 'I'm glad the Jews killed Jesus. I'd do it again.' And someone on the right made a meme of that with a picture of me, like, at the DNC, as if I were giving a press conference. And I get death threats. (Lloyd 2019)

The 'character' Silverman played in her first special *Jesus is Magic* has been described as a cheeky 'Jewish ingénue' (Aarons and Mierowsky 2017b: 163). It is a version of herself designed for the stage: a persona more than a character. The point remains that context is crucial and crucial to context is the notion that persona is constructed. The meme Silverman discusses (see Figure 1) conflates

Figure 1 A meme that decontextualised Sarah Silverman's deliberate comic performance as though she was caught in candid speech. Screenshot by Marc Mierowsky (2023).

what she does on stage with her work as a political activist, a supporter of Bernie Sanders, who spoke for Hillary Clinton in 2016 at the Democratic National Convention in an effort to unify the Democratic base. In presenting a joke she told in 'character' during a special as if it were 'caught' on camera rather than part of a controlled and intricately crafted performance, the meme collapses the distinction between persona and performer. It is a vivid instance of how in our current media environment the remediation of comic speech forces the kind of decontextualisation that makes it increasingly difficult to assert the special conditions of comic licence.

For Silverman, it is not simply a changed media environment that impinges on comic freedom but an audience (no doubt conditioned by this media environment) that fails to understand the nature of comedy. As she defines it, comedy is art, it is performed; while it is often political, it is not political speech and it is a category error to approach it as such:

> It's almost like there's a mutated McCarthy era, where any comic better watch anything they say. If you have a special and someone doesn't agree with every single thing you say on that special . . . you know, [Dave] Chappelle says it at the beginning of his special [*Sticks and Stones*, on Netflix], and he still gets so much . . . for it. I loved it. There were things in it that I did not like. But has there been a special you love and agree with across the board? That's comedy: You overstep. You say things you might not even believe by the time it comes out. You're always changing. It's art. It's not politics. (Lloyd 2019) [italic in the original]

Silverman singles out the beginning of Chappelle's *Sticks and Stones* (2019) as an instance of how comedians might address the difficulties of performing stand-up in an age of 'cancel culture'. The moment she refers to sees Chappelle do an impression of today's audiences:

> [*Puts on a dumb voice.*]
> Uh Duh.
> Hey! Durr!
> If you do anything wrong in your life, duh, and I find out about it, I'm gonna try to take everything away from you, and I don't care when I find out . . . could be today, tomorrow, 15, 20 years from now. If I find out you're fucking-duh-finished . . . .
> That's you.
> That's what the audience sounds like to me
> . . .
> [*Turns to camera and points.*]
> And if you at home watching this on Netflix, remember, b*tch you clicked on my face. (Chapelle 2019)

Chapelle's reminder to the audience watching on Netflix that they chose to click on the special is an attempt to reinscribe the volitional nature of the audience-comedian compact found in theatres and comedy clubs, upon which licence is staked. Set within a bit about members of the public digging up old speech in order to 'cancel' comedians, the gag makes a claim for the function and freedom of comedy. In harking back to an age when he perceived he had greater licence, Chapelle draws attention to the fact that comedians are now held to account for forms of speech, the appearance and circulation of which is beyond their control. In this changed environment, the persona crafted and honed through serial performances is rendered diffuse by the endless, uncontrolled, and decontextualised proliferation of what comedians have said, in multiple venues, in and out of their stage personae.

Silverman has a long history of defending what she and other comedians say on stage. The most famous or indeed infamous incident came in 2001 after Silverman told a joke on the Conan O'Brien show. In an effort to get out of jury duty Silverman tells Conan that she wanted to write something on the intake form like 'I hate ch*nks':

> I wanted to do it, but then I'm like, I don't want people to think I'm racist or something, I just want to get out of jury duty . . .
> So I just filled out the form and I wrote, 'I love ch*nks'.

The joke caused outrage and Guy Aoki, a Japanese American civil rights activist, to publicly accuse Silverman of racism. Silverman refused to apologize and the two were brought together to debate on Bill Maher's show *Politically Incorrect*. Here Silverman retold the joke for the purpose of analysing it. In the process she denuded it of its performative context (Goltz 2017: 54–55). Silverman was unwilling to concede the distinctiveness of comedy. Central to her defence of her satiric methods was a claim that she embodied an ironic persona; she contended that using a slur in this mode does not endorse racism but exposes it, in both its latent and explicit varieties. The fact that she told this joke during an interview and not during a set reveals that the persona she embodies can move from the stage into different modes of performance, complicating its reception. Surveying the controversy, Dustin Bradley Goltz notes that the ironic persona Silverman embodies is 'distinct from the more analytical voice she adopts when writing about it'. There is, in his view, a clear line between the way she performs comedy and how she discusses what that comedy does (Goltz 2017: 55). But as Silverman has branched into Twitter and podcasting, the line between doing comedy and analysing it has tended to blur.

The Politics of Performing Identity

Given Silverman's history of separating persona from comedian, her committed belief that using certain slurs or stereotypes does not necessarily reinforce them, as well as her respect for Dave Chapelle and her 2019 claim that she does not have to like everything in his specials to appreciate his comedy, we have to ask why in 2022 she felt it was necessary to say that his monologue on *Saturday Night Live* was 'hilarious, and brilliant, and winning, and charming and wildly antisemitic' (Silverman 2022). What made her change her assessment of Chapelle? Has his comedy changed? Has hers? Has the world changed so radically in the span of a couple of years? Or has the nature of comic performance? It is difficult to pinpoint a single reason for the shift because there probably isn't one. Chapelle's and Silverman's public interactions are shaped by the fact that the two comedians respect each other and have been friends since Chapelle was seventeen and Silverman was nineteen (Silverman 2019). Both negotiate their identities as minorities on stage and gauge their comic licence in relation to how they understand the place and relative power of these minorities in American society. As such, their identities on stage and in the world are deeply intertwined. Individually and in relation to one another they give an important vantage on how the nature of identity politics forms and deforms comic persona, reshaping ideas of what comics can and cannot say.

Bambi Haggins' incisive study charts the depth and complexity of Chapelle's persona. She characterises Chappelle's style as that of 'story-teller, who with casual and almost lackadaisical candor, pulls you into his world and his logic'; a world whose humour blends 'the sly righteousness and progressive radicalism of Gregory and the outlandish insider truism and gut-busting honesty of [Richard] Pryor.' Haggins traces how Chapelle's persona takes cues from hip hop, tackling marginalisation while at the same time bolstering an autochthonous and community-minded African American culture (2007: 178). In his latest work much of this shift between inward focus on his community and outward focus on the place of his community in society involves a pattern of jokes directed at other minority groups, most notably the LGBTQ community (Balkin 2023).

Across Chapelle's six Netflix specials from 2017–2021, often embedded in larger bits that focus on trans rights, freedom of speech and cancel culture, are jokes about Jews that prefigure the *SNL* monologue. In *The Age of Spin* (2017), Chapelle discusses the loss of sponsorship and endorsement that boxer Manny Pacquaio experienced following his homophobic remarks: 'That's why I don't have a sneaker deal ... if you say something people don't like they'll take your fucking shoes off [*audience laughs*]'. Later in the show Chapelle discusses how he supports gay people and their 'movement' but offers 'some advice from a Negro: "pace yourself"'. The implication which he then spells out is that gay people have achieved more rights far more quickly than Black people. As becomes characteristic in these specials, he homes in on trans people. Following a bit on Caitlyn Jenner, he asks, 'How the fuck are transgender people beating Black people at the discrimination Olympics?'

Chapelle's persona operates on the condition that disempowerment is inversely related to comic licence. As a Black man he has wide latitude. In doing so he repeats a logic he claims to abhor about punching up and punching down.[24] Jokes that punch up to those with more power are permitted. He does not believe he punches down when discussing any other minoritised group. And yet at the same time, he vows that he won't enter into a competition with other minorities over who has suffered more:

> Blacks and Jews do that shit to each other all the time.
> You ever played who suffered more with a Jewish person?
> [*Audience laughs and claps.*]
> It's a tough game
> [*Audience laughs.*]
> Whenever you think you've got the Jewish guy on the ropes, that motherfucker will be like 'well, don't forget about Egypt'.
> Egypt?! God damn, N***a I didn't know we was going all the way back to Egypt.
> [*Audience laughs.*]

Lurking beneath the joke is the idea of historical disjunction. Jewish suffering is not as contemporary as African American suffering. In his interpretation, Jews are no longer on the margins.

A similar premise, albeit expressed more pointedly, underwrites his Jewish jokes in *The Closer* (2021a). While talking about UFOs he pitches a movie idea:

> In my movie idea we find out that these aliens are originally from Earth. That they are from an ancient civilization that achieved interstellar travel and left the Earth thousands of years ago. Some other planet they go to and things go terrible for them in the other planet so they come back to Earth and decide they want to claim the Earth for their very own. It's a pretty good plotline.
> [*Audience yells 'yeah'.*]

---

[24] Chappelle invokes the same logic in *The Closer* when he tells the story of a trans woman who asks him, 'Do you mind not punching down on my people?' Chappelle poses the same question to the LGBTQ community at the end of the special (Balkin 2023: 161–62).

> I call it Space Jews.
> [*Audience claps and laughs.*]

It is a joke about settler-colonialism in Palestine but one that makes light of the Holocaust. The analogy gives him the barest of covers, but just enough. Later in the show he calls back to this joke by telling the true story of a slave in South Carolina who was granted freedom and became a slave owner.

> How can one person that went through slavery perpetuate the same evil on a person that looks just like him. It's mind-blowing. And shockingly they're making a movie about him.
> Ironically [*pauses*], it's called Space Jews.
> [*Audience laughs and whistles.*]

On the face of it the joke is still primarily about Palestine/Israel. But because it is set within the analogy of the slave who becomes slaver it draws into its frame of reference Jewish treatment of Black Americans. Chapelle cultivates an affinity between Black Americans and Palestinians, deploying the history and present suffering of his own people as the basis for, and justification of, his jokes. There are shades here of the notion that is made explicit in the *SNL* monologue that the suffering of Black Americans at the hands of American Jews is justification in and of itself.

In *Equanimity* (2017), Chapelle frames any objection to these kinds of jokes as a function of the polarised nation and the flattening ways it consumes art. He makes a distinction between the crowd in the room and the crowd outside of it: 'It really is the crowd. Not you. I'm talking about the crowd on the big stage. It's too hard to entertain a country whose ears are so brittle'. There is a double justification at work in these specials. Chapelle feels he is permitted by his own identity to joke about everyone, but he also feels licensed by a comedy of an older school, where persona was maintained in the club by a consenting audience who accepted it as 'make-believe', where comic speech was not pressed into new media and forms that flatten and distort its art. It is precisely these two justifications that Sarah Silverman takes him to task on in 2022 following his monologue on *SNL*.

Chapelle's monologue centred on Kanye West, who tweeted on 8 October 2022 that he would go 'death con 3 on JEWISH PEOPLE' (a mangling of DEFCON or defence conditions) and Kyrie Irving, the basketball star who shared a video that denied the Holocaust (Limbong 2022).

West and Irving both buy into the idea that African Americans are descendants of ancient Israelites, a view promoted by the Black Hebrew Israelite movement, and one that often spurs antisemitism. For West, though, it underwrites his confused defence that as an African American 'I actually can't be Anti Semitic' (Limbong 2022). West's tweets and failure to apologise prompted

Adidas to cancel his lucrative sneaker deal. In his *SNL* monologue, Chapelle begins by pretending to read a statement. He pulls a piece of paper out of his pocket and unfolds it. The audience laughs and Chappelle reads:

> I denounce antisemitism in all its forms.
> [*Audience laughs.*]
> And I stand with my friends in the Jewish community.
> [*Folds paper.*]
> And that Kanye is how you buy yourself some time.
> [*Audience laughs and claps.*]
> I gotta tell you guys, I probably been doing this 35 years now and
> early in my career I learned there are two words in the English
> language which you should never say together in sequence and those
> words are 'THE' and 'JEWS'.
> [*Audience laughs.*]
> Never heard someone do good after they said that (Deggans 2022).

Silverman's response came a few weeks later. She had taken time off from *The Sarah Silverman Podcast* to recover from surgery to remove her tonsils and was deeply reluctant to broach the topic of Chapelle's monologue. When she did, she examined the underside of comic licence, pointing to how humour can smooth the path for prejudice:

> I'm sure that most people who watched it hating Jews was not their take away you know because they were busy laughing at all the other stuff and the brilliant stuff but I will tell you that Jews for the most part were hypersensitive to it just like any minority is going to be more keenly aware of the hatreds and little aggressions against them and there were a bunch of Jewish jokes in there that were fucking hilarious but that's what made the antisemitism in it so scary it bolstered it you know its like Hannah Einbinder who is so brilliant wrote about it [on Twitter] and she pointed out it's two truths and a lie that bigotry is always couched in a couple of true things to bolster a big lie
>
> And for me two moments of his monologue made me worry that um ignite more violence against Jews which is a crazy and totally rational fear that I have and the two moments were the part about Kyrie Irving and the last line. (Silverman 2022)

The first bit Silverman cites is Chapelle's response to the attempt of the NBA to push Irving to apologise:

> And the NBA told him he should apologise and he was slow to apologise and then the list of demands to get back in their good graces got longer and longer and this is where, you know, I draw the line. I know the Jewish people have

been through terrible things all over the world but.. [*stutters*] but you can't
blame that on Black Americans you just can't
[*one audience member woos*].

Silverman who, like Chapelle, is a master of the craft of stand-up, analyses what
she thinks he is doing here:

> You know he kind of like Jimmy Stewart stutters at the end to give it a little
> uh folksy truth-telling charm I guess [*Silverman laughs*]. You know Kanye
> said he wanted to kill the Jews and Kyrie posted a movie that promotes the
> ideals that put Jews in actual mortal danger. But fuck like the idea of
> calling out massively influential zillionaire superstars for posting lies and
> promoting hatred of Jews all Jews like we're a monolith is the Jews
> blaming their troubles on Black Americans is fucking insane. I can't
> believe I have to say this [*chuckles*] you know each of them individually
> have more followers just on Instagram than there are Jews in the world.
> Jews aren't punching down here by calling out antisemitism. Fucking good
> grief.

Silverman invokes the strictures against punching down, by which Chapelle
justified his own jokes about trans people (despite attempting to disavow the
idea wholesale). That Silverman makes space for a critique using this limit even
though 'calling out antisemitism' is not comic speech exposes a clear break-
down in the divisions between comic performance and everyday speech and persona and performer.

Silverman also takes issue with the final line of the monologue:

> And the other thing Dave said that sent a chill down my spine was the way he
> ended his monologue which is he said [*plays clip*], 'I hope they don't take
> anything away from me' [*audience laughs*], 'whoever they are'.
> Silverman: and there right there Chapelle made himself bulletproof because if
> he faces a single consequence you know who to blame.

In the excerpt Chapelle echoes his Pacquiao joke from *The Age of Spin*. There is
an unmistakeable difference, however. In the earlier joke, it was an undifferen-
tiated crowd that caused Pacquiao's cancellation. In the case of the monologue,
as Silverman points out, the 'they' is clearly 'the Jews', the very collocation
Chapelle notes he cannot use. The Jews become the power lurking behind the
brittle, sensitive crowd. As the podcast goes on, Silverman delves into why she
thinks Chapelle is wrong. In her account, he is not punching up as a Black
comedian (when he jokes about Jewish power and influence) and is mistaken to
think that the 'anything goes' of comic licence should allow antisemitism to
pass without consequence. As she makes her points, Silverman describes how
every time she tries to push back against antisemitism, Twitter users flood her

wall with pictures of herself in blackface from *The Sarah Silverman Program*, in an episode where she fights over who has it worse, Black people or Jews, 'which to be honest still resonates'. She accounts for her choices without justifying them: her blackface was 'racist by design because it was an episode about racism and I played the racist'. She performed the program as the ironic persona from her stand-up. Still, she concedes it was ignorant and she would not do blackface again. Set against her other defences, there is in Silverman's mind a distinction between blackface and her use of the slur 'ch*nks'. This line seems to be as much about personal judgement as social standards. But as she draws the conversation back to the notion that 'anything goes' in comedy, she offers her friend Dave Chapelle a caveat:

> There is a caveat to anything goes … there's one caveat. In comedy there is one rule to anything goes and that rule is and it's the one rule of [comic] roasts is that you must love the person you're roasting or it does not work.
>
> …
>
> This overly sensitive time will pass when and if we live in a post race society where the structure of our society in the bedrock of our system is not founded in racism. (Silverman 2022)

In Silverman's utopian vision all jokes can be told. The reverse of this is that until that utopian time, it becomes increasingly difficult to assert, prove, or discern any underlying love when identity comes into play. In a cultural moment where we are more aware of systemic and structural racism than ever before, jokes about one minority group even when told by another test the limits of licence. The question that remains is whether comic persona is still a useful category when its operation becomes so bound up with the politics of identity that it allows for neither ironic detachment nor love.

3 Comic Licence

This section updates a foundational concept in stand-up comedy studies: the live-audience contract of comic licence, where a comedian must keep control of the room to succeed. Stated simply, comic licence is the comedian's permission to speak, as granted by the audience. Mid twentieth-century Jewish and African American comedians such as Lenny Bruce and Richard Pryor both established and overstepped the boundaries of this genre convention, which continues to inform how many comedians conceptualise what they do. Some comedians such as Judy Gold, Chris Rock, and Dave Chappelle understand comic licence as both threatened by and superior to contemporary frameworks for what they feel they are 'allowed' to say, such as 'cancel culture' and 'political correctness'. These rhetorical and cultural phenomena are especially pronounced on social media platforms and have become a central preoccupation for a subset of comedians, most prominently Rock and Chappelle. In this context, while contemporary comedy is still performed for live audiences, the widespread dissemination of and responses to stand-up across media platforms complicates the idea of comic licence for both comedians and scholarship. Who, in these circumstances, is the audience, and what is the comedian's contract with them?

Bruce and Pryor kept faith to the belief that their wit and insight served a social need and a higher moral purpose. Both built their sets from the premise that comic licence gave them the freedom to speak truth to power. The cultural and media contexts in which licence operates have changed: while Bruce and Pryor were counterculture figures who tended to offend and be censored by the state or by network executives, as Gold points out, 'it's no longer just right-wing conservatives who are silencing comedians and artists. Attempts at censorship are now coming from the so-called progressive left as well' (2020: 19). While there is a degree of truth to the idea of the progressive left as the new 'morals police' (Gold 2020: 18), the type of censorship has changed: comedians deemed offensive might be hounded on social media platforms or faced with demands for their specials to be removed from Netflix, but they are not being arrested.[25] In some ways, the polarised public discourse of social media culture is more like comic licence than traditional censorship, if social media users are understood as an extended audience with the right to respond in the moment. On the other hand, to the extent that attempts to cancel or boycott performers pressure networks or media companies not to platform comedians' work, this is more like a private censorship campaign (see ACLU 2006).

Many comedians align licence with free speech – the idea that there is nothing they are 'not allowed' to say. In fact, licence is delimited by what a given audience will accept rather than specific 'allowed' or 'not allowed' speech (see Balkin 2023: 155). As Aarons and Mierowsky (2017a: 166) note, the comedian's permission to speak 'is the product of negotiation: between performer and audience, between communicating intention and having that intention realized'. Comic licence depends on the audience's shared values, though 'the consensus on what's suitable and what's not can change' (Double 2014: 264) over time or even from one performance to the next. Moreover,

---

[25] See also Nesteroff 2023: 15.

the audience's shared values are not only pre-existing; the comedian helps to build what they share in the room, or across a career. A comedian might accomplish the former through a callback, a joke that refers to one previously told in the set; discussion of current events; or various forms of storytelling that create a shared context that influences reception. Oliver Double (2014: 262) gives a good example of building what an audience shares across a career when he discusses how audiences expect English comedian Jo Brand to say outrageous things; this is part of her established persona. She is therefore 'licensed to shock'. Audiences can challenge or revoke a comedian's licence to speak by heckling, refusing to laugh, booing, or walking out (Aarons and Mierowsky 2017a: 160; Balkin 2023: 155). If the comedian succeeds in regaining control of the room, they retain their licence; if not, the licence is revoked.

In contrast to contemporary comedians who claim their free speech is threatened by leftist political correctness, Rebecca Krefting (2014: 21) identifies a particular mode that she terms 'charged humour', where the creation of a shared context is intended to have wide-reaching social effects. Charged humour is that which 'seeks to represent the underrepresented, to empower and affirm marginalized communities and identities and to edify and mobilize their audiences'. Though Krefting does not refer to licence explicitly, the framework she brings to bear echoes its basic dynamic. By virtue of the intersection of their identity and positive, empowering social intent certain comedians can joke about minoritised communities without suffering the opprobrium of the left. For Krefting, this is because their humour seeks a form of 'cultural citizenship', bolstering that community's 'sense of belonging' and internal cohesiveness while also cultivating solidarity and identification by those outside the community (71). The success of this humour is hard to measure, but like the notion of licence, the immediate reaction is key: 'Laughter signals both identification and agreement'; silence, on the other hand, shows an audience that is not yet willing to identify with the performer's world view or change the way they view that performer's subject position (98). Krefting takes a long view of this dynamic, seeking ways to trace the effects of charged humour over time. In our view licence is implicit to the working of charged humour and remains a good metric for understanding the performance and reception of stand-up by comedians across a range of social identities. Moreover, while Krefting is right to note that comedians who perform charged humour risk less economic viability due to their polarising content (232), we discuss several comedians whose political content and even cancellation have added to their fame, generating opportunities for additional Netflix specials, for example.

Traditionally, comedians and audiences negotiate comic licence in a live venue; as a result, 'the room' becomes a metonym for the audience. This relationship between licence and the live venue has implications for how comedians understand their work. Hannah Gadsby put this succinctly in a 2017 interview with Australian journalist Leigh Sales, who suggested that even if audiences had rejected *Nanette*, Gadsby still would have found performing the show 'personally a useful exercise'. Gadsby disagreed, noting that if 'it had been rejected in the room, no, I would have stopped, I would have adjusted, because that's what I do. That's what being a comedian is: you read the room' (Sales 2017; Balkin 2020b: 81–82). Chris Rock likewise understands licence as fundamental to comedy and suggests that it makes contemporary cancel culture redundant. 'When you're a comedian', he notes in a 2021 interview, 'when the audience doesn't laugh, we get the message. You don't really have to cancel us because we get the message. They're not laughing'. According to Rock, cancel culture is therefore 'disrespectful' to the live audience, whose role is already to decide what is acceptable for the comedian to say (McCarthy 2021; Balkin 2023: 155). In other words, Rock invokes the understanding of comic licence that emerges from mid twentieth-century comedians such as Bruce and Pryor to assert that comedy already has its own system for determining what comedians are allowed to say.

As Balkin (2023) argues in 'On Quitting: Dave Chappelle's *The Closer* and Hannah Gadsby's *Nanette*', Chappelle extends Rock's understanding of comic licence to a paradigm that enables better communication than cancel culture. Chappelle does this through two stories about Daphne Dorman, a transgender comedian who, Chappelle claims, was hounded by the woke left on Twitter for defending Chappelle's jokes about trans people in 2019, in the wake of his Netflix special *Sticks and Stones*. In *Sticks and Stones*' epilogue, Chappelle discusses how Dorman laughed at the trans jokes in his show; he represents her as a counterpoint to over-sensitive PC culture (Chappelle 2019; Balkin 2023: 159).[26] Dorman subsequently defended Chappelle on Twitter when he was criticised for transphobia (Dorman 29 August 2019). She also advertised her association with Chappelle in her Twitter bio, which still posthumously reads, 'Yep, I'm the Daphne that Dave Chappelle is talking about in Sticks and Stones' (Dorman 2019). In his next special, *The Closer* (2021a), Chappelle falsely implies that being dragged on

---

[26] At the time of writing, the twenty-minute epilogue to *Sticks and Stones* is not available as part of the special on Netflix in Australia but is available on YouTube at /www.youtube.com/watch?v=wdOa73BzsSk.

Twitter for defending him may have contributed to Dorman's subsequent suicide. We say 'falsely' because this aspect of Chappelle's story is fictionalised; there is no evidence that Dorman was attacked by the woke left (see Hobbes 2021; Balkin 2023: 158).[27] As an alternative to woke cancel culture Chappelle offers the story of the time Dorman opened for him in San Francisco, bombed, but then won over the crowd through her handling of a heckler during Chappelle's set. In response to the heckler asking, 'Does the carpet match the drapes?' Dorman replied, 'Sir, I don't have carpets I have hardwood floors' (Chappelle 2021a). The audience, won over by Dorman's joke, was back on her side and gave her a standing ovation at the end of the show. Chappelle presents this moment as more effective than politically correct leftist rhetoric, noting that Dorman 'didn't say anything about pronouns. She didn't say anything about me being in trouble' (Chappelle 2021a). The anecdote is a persuasive endorsement of the live-audience contract of comic licence: Dorman fought with funniness and won the audience over for the remainder of the show, even if many of them did not share her experience.

The Extended Audience

Contemporary scholarship in audience studies has troubled the assumption that audiences are passive whereas performers are active (Rancière 2011, Heim 2016, Sedgman 2017). This has always been clear in stand-up, which emerged from the vaudeville tradition of direct communication with an outwardly responsive audience (Jenkins 1992: 31–32) rather than from the modernist conventions of the fourth wall, darkened auditorium, and quiet spectators. It is modernist conventions of spectatorship that inform assumptions about passive audiences – and, of course, these less animated audiences still have their own practices, behaviours, and performances: listening, applauding, falling asleep, queuing for the toilet or a glass of wine at intermission, and so on. But if all audiences are to some degree performers, stand-up not only emphasises but also relies heavily on active aspects of spectatorship by responding in real time to what is happening in the room: the audience's laughter is part of the rhythm of jokes; a comedian might get an easy laugh by calling out latecomers; and 'crowd work' refers to the practice of engaging with audience members during the performance (e.g., asking, 'What do you do for a living?'), to name a few examples. If an audience refuses to play by withholding laughter or challenges the comedian by heckling, the comedian must respond in real time to regain control of the room.

---

[27]   Balkin (2023) unpacks the implications of this fictionalisation in Chappelle's show, which is both conventional in comedy and disingenuous in the context of the 'serious' point Chappelle uses the story to make.

Sometimes stand-up audience members overstep their conventional roles. Chappelle's story about Dorman is an unusual example of comic licence in that while she was on stage as his opening act – which Chappelle (2021a) described as a 'stinker of a show' – when she won the audience over with her joke about hardwood floors, Dorman was technically a heckler herself. As Chappelle tells it, Dorman good-naturedly stuck around after she bombed and took a seat in the audience where, drunk, she started talking to him during his set. It was then that the audience, annoyed by Dorman's interruptions, began to heckle her in turn. Once Dorman got her zinger in and won over the audience, Chappelle actively incorporated her into his show, which 'became like a conversation between a Black man and a white trans woman' (Chappelle 2021a). As a celebrity who held the stage Chappelle had greater power in this conversation, though Dorman found him generous and was happy to collaborate with him.[28] Thus, Chappelle's story of Dorman's heckling and being heckled remains a successful (if unusual) example of negotiating comic licence. The example shows, moreover, how negotiation does not imply equality.

Moments when audience members overstep their conventional roles in this negotiation are not always so felicitous. For example, at the 2022 Oscars, host Chris Rock's performance was interrupted and overshadowed by the moment known colloquially as 'the slap'. Rock makes a joke about audience member Jada Pinkett Smith's bald head: 'GI Jane 2, can't wait to see it' (*Entertainment Tonight* 2022). The camera cuts away to Pinkett Smith and her husband Will Smith for their reactions. Although Will Smith initially laughs, Pinkett Smith, who has alopecia, rolls her eyes. Will Smith then walks on stage and slaps Rock for joking about his wife. Smith leaves the stage and Rock tries to recover a comic tone, saying, 'Oh wow . . . Will Smith just smacked the shit out of me'. From his seat, clearly angry, Smith twice orders Rock to 'keep my wife's name out your fucking mouth'. From the stage, Rock conciliates: 'I'm going to, OK . . . . That was . . . the greatest night in the history of television . . . OK'. Some laughter follows Rock's attempt to get things back on track, but he is clearly shaken and the tone in the room is uncertain. More than one attendee at the live event noted they were unclear 'if it was staged or a joke at first' (*Entertainment Tonight* 2022). This uncertainty points to how the controversy that comedy inspires also frequently scripts its subject matter.

A Hollywood awards show is not a typical stand-up audience, though it is one of the contexts in which people who may not be comedy fans typically

---

[28] There were many popular media critiques of Chappelle's use of Dorman in *The Closer*, including that Chappelle exploits Dorman's death in the show, but Dorman consistently defended Chappelle on Twitter. See Balkin 2023: 156–61, which also discusses Chappelle's fictionalisation of the woke mob that purportedly hounded Dorman.

encounter stand-up comedians. The practice of cutting away to get audience reactions is common to filmed stand-up specials and award shows. The camera's position and editing create a shared viewing experience for the otherwise dispersed television or streaming audience; in contrast, the live audience, who are seated in different parts of the venue, will see and hear slightly different versions of the show. For example, Madeline Parry, the director of the Netflix version of Gadsby's *Nanette*, notes that the practice of cutting away to the audience breaks the tension in a traditional comedy special; Parry's choice not to show audience reactions in the filmed version of *Nanette* thus supported Gadsby's aim of refusing to relieve the audience's tension in order to make a point about how comedy works (Giuffre 2021: 36). One of the ways cutting to the audience can break the tension is by a kind of affective tuning: a television or Netflix viewer does not experience the affective contagion of proximity to other bodies in the live venue, but their response to comic material is still influenced by seeing and hearing others laughing (or not laughing). At an awards show broadcast the live audience, many of whom are celebrities, are unusually aware of themselves as both performers and spectators. Taylor Swift skilfully navigated this dynamic when 2024 Golden Globes host Jo Koy made a joke about the frequency with which Swift features in cut-away shots at NFL games, which she attends in support of her boyfriend, Kansas City Chiefs player Travis Kelce. Koy (Shared News 2024) said, 'The big difference between the Golden Globes and the NFL? On the Golden Globes, we have fewer camera shots of Taylor Swift'. The camera cut to Swift, who pressed her lips together and took a sip of her drink. Swift's (Woodroof 2024) 'devastating look' became an 'instant meme' that emphasised Koy's failure to win over either the live room or the extended mediatised audience.

Smith, in contrast, succeeded in derailing Rock, but he did so in a way that caused consternation and dissensus in the live and online audiences. *The New Yorker* writer Michael Schulman noted a split between these audiences: 'On social media, viewers were studying footage and taking sides, deconstructing the moment in terms of race, class, and trauma. But at the Dolby the mood was mostly bewilderment' (2022). A thread from @latimes' (*Los Angeles Times* 2022) Twitter account shows that plenty of online viewers also thought the slap was a joke or a fake. Many thought Smith had every right to defend his wife and others condemned his use of violence. Some called for legal action against Smith. Many were preoccupied by the fact that Smith laughed at Rock's joke before seeing that Pinkett Smith was not amused. Smith's action was an individual attempt to revoke Rock's licence to speak that wildly overstepped the conventions of audience behaviour, causing uncertainty in the live audience and controversy among the extended mediatised audience. While the slap was initially mistaken for a performance, unlike conventional modes of revoking licence such as heckling or booing, the action Smith took cannot be called negotiation. Had Smith simply walked out, he might have won the live Hollywood audience and/or the extended mediatised audience to his side – audiences might have decided Rock had crossed a line by making fun of Pinkett Smith's alopecia. A walkout would therefore have been a way of signalling that negotiation was over (Smith was no longer willing to listen or be present) that could still have performed a negotiating function more broadly by influencing other audience members. As events transpired, Smith succeeded in temporarily derailing the performance, which Rock could not easily bring back to a comic register. But Smith's belated humourlessness and subsequent violence also became the event in a way that resulted in his resignation from the Academy and his banning from all Academy events for ten years. In overstepping the audience's prerogative to revoke Rock's licence to speak, then, Smith found himself subject to an organisational revocation of his right to be present.

The slap galvanised another genre of performance, the celebrity apology, across a range of media: at the live broadcast when Smith subsequently won the Oscar for best actor, on Instagram in March 2022 (@willsmith 2022), and then again in a YouTube video in July 2022 (Lee 2022a). As Goltz (2024: 17) notes, social media call-out culture has increased demand for such apologies, which mark a site of struggle over competing social and generational values. Rock, meanwhile, incorporated the incident into his 2023 Netflix special, *Selective Outrage*, which he begins by noting that he will try to do the show without offending anyone. 'You know, anybody that says "words hurt" has never been punched in the face', Rock continues. This distinction between physical and verbal harm echoes Chappelle's *Sticks and Stones* (2019), the title of which is from the old children's rhyme, 'sticks and stones will break my bones but words will never hurt me'. Rock's show thus joins Chappelle's late work in taking aim at cancel culture, political correctness, and the hypocrisy of what in this special Rock calls 'selective outrage', where people choose to be offended by some things and not others. The framing of Rock's special, which begins and ends with material about Smith, suggests the intertextuality of contemporary comedy specials that respond not only to political debates and events, but to the iterations of those debates and events across media and other comedy shows. Seen in this light, Rock's *Selective Outrage* might also be understood as an attempt to regain control of the room, where the extended 'room' encompasses a different venue (the Hippodrome Theatre in Baltimore, Maryland), the dispersed mediatised Netflix audience, and the popular and social media audience whose commentary constitutes the larger debate and reception environment.

As is already apparent, contemporary comedy circulates across a range of visual and discursive media, often in truncated or de- and recontextualised forms. A recorded performance becomes the de facto version of record, eliding the ways comedy shows change across a run. This has been the case for some time with recorded comedy specials and albums, which have circulated for decades on television and other media such as vinyl, VHS tapes, and DVDs (see Krefting 2014: 71–72). In mediatised comedy the 'room' is still present, in that stand-up is still performed in front of a live audience, but when those performances are disseminated on televised, streaming, or social media platforms, the live audience is only a fraction of the total audience. As Goltz (2017: 94) notes,

> While the text of the mediated event may now be distributed in a form that appears more static and fixed, it is encountering an expanding network of mediated audiences that are actively negotiating and reproducing meanings in participatory and geographically unrestricted ways and exponential contexts. With the advent of the Internet and social media, the very notion of context has seismically shifted in ever-increasing ways.

The live audience's recorded reactions still influence the performance's reception, in that those who watch recorded versions will often see or hear the live audience's laughter (or lack thereof). What has changed with the advent of streaming and social media are the platforms and rapidity with which viewers and users encounter, comment on, and recontextualise performances.[29]

While Kliph Nesteroff (2023: 17–18) is right to note comedy provoked outrage well before the social media age, we argue that the ways comedians and audiences perform on social media platforms demonstrate the need to revise the live audience contract of comic licence. For example, after transgender Netflix employees staged a walkout protesting transphobic content in *The Closer*, Chappelle (2021b) posted a video to Instagram of a live appearance where he addressed his purported cancellation. We say 'purported' because the cancellation was a controversy in which Chappelle stayed highly visible and successful, and because trans Netflix employees were not actually lobbying for his show to be removed from the streaming service.[30] In the video, Chappelle proposed that he was willing to meet with members of the 'trans community'

---

[29] See also C. Borum Chattoo. (2023). *The Revolution Will Be Hilarious: Comedy for Social Change and Civic Power.* New York: New York University Press on comedy's role in 'the participatory traits of the postmillennial media era' (2023: 5). Where our focus is on controversy, Borum Chattoo's is on activism.

[30] Trans Netflix employees' demands focused instead on how references to and imagery from Chappelle's show impacted them in the workplace and on supporting trans and nonbinary content on the platform (Carras 2021; Balkin 2023 note 4).

who were upset by *The Closer*, 'but I have some conditions: first of all, you cannot come if you have not watched my special from beginning to end. You must come to a place of my choosing at a time of my choosing. And thirdly, you must admit that Hannah Gadsby is not funny'. There are several sets of addressees for Chappelle's statement: (1) his live audience, who laugh in the video; (2) his Instagram followers, who performed their support for the video with 301,369 likes (as of June 2023); and (3) woke trans people and other lefties, who he is trolling in a manner characteristic of his late work (see Balkin 2023). Out.com writer Mey Rude (2021) walks right into Chappelle's trap when they ask, 'So who exactly is this "trans community" Chappelle has extended this invitation to? Can any trans person who meets his requirements talk to him? Does he think there's a Trans Pope or Trans President who can speak for us?' These would be excellent questions if Chappelle had been speaking in earnest. In the context of a video about, in Chappelle's own words, cancel culture and what he is allowed to say, the facetious conditions for dialogue make fun of supposed leftie rules about who can say what and under what conditions even as the live audience licenses Chappelle's speech with its laughter. Chappelle's performance does not actually invite dialogue from trans people; instead, it addresses and constructs an absent audience of woke lefties, including social media users and popular media writers like Rude, and invites them to be humourless. In other words, while Rock and Chappelle are invested in and assert comic licence's superiority to other frameworks for allowing or restricting comedians' speech, Chappelle is also adept at deploying facetious or bad-faith versions of these other frameworks (cancel culture, political correctness) in ways that trigger the social scripts he rejects.

Musk Live

In December 2022, Twitter owner and CEO Elon Musk appeared on stage in Chappelle and Rock's show at Chase Center in San Francisco. Following sets in which the two comedians discussed cancel culture and the Will Smith slap incident, Chappelle asked the 18,000-strong arena crowd to 'make some noise for the richest man in the world' (*Guardian News* 2022). The noise they made was booing. Chappelle joked, 'It sounds like some of them people you fired must be in the audience' (Guardian News 2022). Musk initiated his acquisition of Twitter in April 2022 and concluded it in October of the same year. His stated motive was that he was a 'free speech absolutist' (Perrigo 2022). While Twitter had previously largely aligned with this ethos, increasing harassment and misinformation on the site led the company to introduce greater content moderation, with the signal event being the permanent suspension of former President

Donald Trump's account in January 2021 when he attempted to overturn the results of the US presidential election. Musk's interest in the platform was to roll back much of the moderation on the logic that free speech serves democracy, though research shows that 'sites that privilege free speech above all else tend to result in spaces where civic discourse is drowned out by harassment, restricting participation to a privileged few' (Perrigo 2022). Following his acquisition of the company, in November 2022 Musk laid off about half of Twitter's 7,500 employees, a significant number of whom lived in San Francisco, where it was headquartered.

Ironically, in this live appearance Musk embodied a social media platform that, like comedy, has become a flashpoint for public debates about free speech and cancel culture. The audience's live booing was a localised re-instantiation of traditional comic licence (the audience revoked Musk's licence to speak). Chappelle's motive for bringing Musk on stage is puzzling: although in the moment he claimed he had made a 'deal' with Musk for the 'first comedy club on Mars' (Mendoza 2022), this was clearly a joke. It seems likeliest that Chappelle brought Musk on as a fellow advocate for free speech and an opponent of leftist content moderation. Perhaps he merely miscalculated the audience's response to Musk, but one of Chappelle's core skills is a finely tuned understanding of who his audience is and how to keep them on side. Indeed, journalist Josh Koehn (2022), who attended the show, observed that Chappelle 'seemed to have no plan beyond bringing one of the most polarising figures in the world onstage', but also 'clearly knew what he was doing in bringing Musk onstage'. Musk did not have anything special to say or do during his appearance: some waves, a double fist-pump, a shrug, and a few inane comments ('I'm rich, b*tch!' – a quote from an old Chappelle sketch; 'What should I do, Dave?'; 'I think we're in a simulation') were it. In our opinion, he was there to be booed (whether he knew it or not). Perhaps it was a simple publicity stunt, or perhaps Chappelle was interested in splitting his audience. Regardless, it was a moment where the live 'room' silenced a purported free speech absolutist in ways that seemed to take him by surprise.

But social media commentary after the fact also showed how layers of mediatisation can change the event and its significance. The next day, Musk tweeted, 'Technically, it was 90% cheers & 10% boos (except during quiet periods), but, still, that's a lot of boos, which is a first for me in real life (frequent on Twitter). It's almost as if I've offended SF's unhinged leftists . . . but nahhh' (Mendoza 2022). Musk's tweet has since been deleted. The deletion and the capture of the tweet for posterity in spite of deletion show how public speech on social media platforms is both subject to editorial revision and difficult to contain, once published. In contrast to Musk's tweet, videos of the event uploaded to YouTube (Guardian News 2022; Wilda 2022) suggest there were more boos than cheers. The characterisation of Chappelle and Rock's audience as 'unhinged leftists' is curious, as supposed woke mobs of unhinged leftists are the targets, rather than the audiences, of their respective shows. Or are they? Again, Chappelle is adept at addressing more than one audience. Generally, as in *The Closer* or in his facetious conditions for meeting with trans people offended by it, this has consisted of making the live audience laugh while baiting social and popular media commentators outside the room. But at Chase Center, with Musk on stage, Chappelle began to bait at least some sections of his live audience: 'All you people booing', he said, 'and I'm just pointing out the obvious—are in terrible seats' (Wilda 2022). The implication was that the audience members who booed resented Musk for being rich. Although there was some laughter at Chappelle's joke, the booing continued, seemingly from all parts of the stadium (it is hard to tell in recordings). What interests us here is the way Chappelle responds to live censure by attempting to split the audience and characterise part of it as a particular demographic. Musk enacts a version of this in his tweet, which retroactively casts 10 per cent of the live Chase Center audience as unhinged leftists rather than poor people. In other words, both Chappelle and Musk respond to censure by attempting to define who the audience – and, crucially, a fictionalised minority of the audience – is. In this way, they attempt to change what the event means.

Comic licence, we have said, is the comedian's permission to speak as granted by the audience. But the comedian also constructs who the audience is, a process that depends on the performer's skill and the audience's pre-existing sense of themselves as individuals and/or as members of a range of types of community. Free speech debates about comedy, then, are misleading because comic speech was never free, but was always negotiated. Some of the ways of negotiating have changed as the 'room' has expanded across digital and social media. 'Who is the audience?' is a question that always had more than one answer, in that audiences would change from night to night, and from venue to venue. But the question is now more complicated because streamed and socially mediatised comedy has many more audiences: those in the live rooms in which the comic developed their material; those in the live room at the recorded event; those who watch the recorded event, often alone, at different times and in different places; and those who comment on the event in popular and social media in ways that recirculate audio-visual and textual excerpts from the performance. There is therefore more than one contract between audience and performer in play and the kinds of speech and fiction-alisation conventional to stand-up sometimes have different meanings or effects as a result.

Conclusion: Gender Agenda/Banana Palace

We began this Element by proposing that comedy scholarship can respond to the changed contexts in which stand-up circulates by answering three basic questions: what is the comedian's persona, how does that persona establish the comedian's licence to speak, and how do (mediatised) performance contexts shape and complicate the audience's contract with the comedian? We have modelled this approach in the preceding sections in hope of producing a fuller understanding of how comic controversies script and are scripted by public speech. In so doing we have shown how contemporary comedy is both continuous with foundational conventions of modern stand-up and subject to new modes of distribution and spectatorship that complicate the comedian's contract with the expanded audience. As media platforms and modes of distribution change, and as comedians continually renegotiate their roles as public figures, the questions we ask about comedy will need to shift again. For now, though, we have seen no sign of the demise of the conventions of persona and licence and Netflix continues to pump out comedy specials, some of which are in clear conversation with public controversies as well as other comedians. Indeed, as we were completing the manuscript, *Hannah Gadsby's Gender Agenda*, a special featuring seven genderqueer comedians, premiered on Netflix. The special presents trans and genderqueer voices in comedy even as it references public discourse about the 'gay agenda', a term popularised by the American religious right in the 1990s. In the opening, Gadsby (2024a) references the Chappelle controversy when they quip, 'The last time Netflix brought this many trans people together, it was for a protest. So, progress!'

In contrast, at a December 2023 show in Melbourne, Gadsby commented on their celebrity and its impact on their comedy: 'I don't want to be bigger', they noted, 'I want to be weirder'. The show that followed, *Banana Palace*, did contain a now-signature rant or two, but it was not especially controversial and it included Gadsby reading a series of unsent fan letters to Barbara Streisand. It was weird and charming, and it was structured by one of Gadsby's preoccupations as a neurodivergent person, an aspect of their updated persona. Much of the humour arose from Gadsby's 'rambling, awkwardly overfamiliar' (Woodhead 2023) mode of address to Streisand, which raised questions about epistolarity and performance conventions: to whom were they speaking, and why in this way, when they read us the letters and asked the live audience for feedback? A show staged in December is generally a trial run for the Melbourne International Comedy Festival, which is held in March and April. But *Woof!* (2024b) was an almost entirely different show to *Banana Palace*: Gadsby noted they had a panic attack the week before the start of the festival and changed it all. In *Woof!* Gadsby discussed their uncertainty about who their audience is now that they are famous. Asked by an audience member who had attended *Banana Palace* what had happened to the letters to Streisand, Gadsby said they were still writing them, but they weren't reading them to us anymore. *Banana Palace* showed Gadsby sidelining the kinds of public debate and social media scripts that made them an international celebrity while still clearly thinking through issues of celebrity, audience, and what is at stake in modes of address in stand-up. This is to affirm that the ways mediatised public controversies prime people to understand comedy can expand the genre as well as prescribe it, even in the work of a single performer. It is more difficult to see whether and how such genre experiments might change public speech, though in the difficulty lies some of the potential for change.

References

Aarons, D. and Mierowsky, M. (2014). Obscenity, Dirtiness and Licence in Jewish Comedy. *Comedy Studies*, 5, 165–77. https://doi.org/10.1080/2040610X.2014.967017.

Aarons, D. and Mierowsky, M. (2017a). How to Do Things with Jokes: Speech Acts in Standup Comedy. *The European Journal of Humour Research*, 5(4), 158–68. https://doi.org/10.7592/EJHR2017.5.4.aarons.

Aarons, D. and Mierowsky, M. (2017b). Public Conscience of 'the Chosen People': Sarah Silverman in the Wake of Lenny Bruce. *Comedy Studies*, 8(2), 154–66. https://doi.org/10.1080/2040610X.2017.1343272.

Aarons, D. and Mierowsky, M. (2025). Jewish American Stand-up. In O. Double, ed., *The Cambridge Companion to Stand-up Comedy*. Cambridge: Cambridge University Press.

ABC Close Up Report (1961). Walk in My Shoes. www.youtube.com/watch?v=082Z9w1BeqU.

ACLU. (2006). What Is Censorship? www.aclu.org/documents/what-censorship.

Auslander, P. (2008). *Liveness: Performance in a Mediatized Culture*. New York: Routledge.

Balkin, S. (2020a). Deadpan and Comedy Theory. In Matthew Kaiser, ed., *A Cultural History of Comedy*, Vol. 5. London: Bloomsbury, 43–66.

Balkin, S. (2020b). The Killjoy Comedian: Hannah Gadsby's Nanette. *Theatre Research International*, 45, 72–85. https://doi.org/10.1017/S0307883319000592.

Balkin, S. (2021). Transporting Humour: Artemus Ward and American Comedy in Britain. In Gilli Bush-Bailey and Kate Flaherty, eds., *Touring Performance and Global Exchange 1850–1960: Making Tracks*. London: Routledge, 208–17. https://doi.org/10.4324/9781003055860-13.

Balkin, S. (2023). On Quitting: Dave Chappelle's The Closer and Hannah Gadsby's Nanette. *TDR: The Drama Review*, 67, 149–66. https://doi.org/10.1017/S1054204322000958.

Baym, G. (2005). The Daily Show: Discursive Integration and the Reinvention of Political Journalism. *Political Communication* 22(3), 259–76.

Bennett, A. (2019). Allelujah! *London Review of Books*, 41, No 1. www.lrb.co.uk/the-paper/v41/n01/alan-bennett/diary.

Bilici, M. (2010). Muslim Ethnic Comedy: Inversions of Islamophobia. In Andrew Shryock, ed., *Islamophobia/Islamophilia: Beyond the Politics of Enemy and Friend.* Bloomington: Indiana University Press, 195–208.

Black, S. (2020). Tristram Shandy, Essayist. In Thomas Karshan and Kathryn Murphy, eds., *On Essays: Montaigne to the Present.* Oxford: Oxford University Press, 132–49. https://doi.org/10.1093/oso/9780198707868.001.0001.

Borum Chattoo, C. (2023). *The Revolution Will Be Hilarious: Comedy for Social Change and Civic Power.* New York: New York University Press.

Bradley, L. (2018). Did Hannah Gadsby Just Subtweet Her Nastiest Critics at the Emmys? *Vanity Fair.* www.vanityfair.com/hollywood/2018/09/emmys-2018-hannah-gadsby-jokes.

Carras, C. (2021). Fed up with Chappelle fallout, Netflix Employees Are Leading a Walkout Today in L.A. *Los Angeles Times.* www.latimes.com/entertainment-arts/tv/story/2021-10-20/netflix-walkout-dave-chappelle-special-trans-employees.

Chappell, D. (2017). *The Age of Spin.* Netflix.

Chappell, D. (2019). *Sticks and Stones.* Netflix.

Chappell, D. (2021a). *The Closer.* Netflix.

Chappelle, D. (2021b). 'Screening of "Untitled" Dave Chappelle Documentary directed by Oscar winning filmmakers Julia Reichert and Steve Bognar. Plus Live . . . ' . www.instagram.com/tv/CVde5tAFT4H/.

Cohen, J. (1987). *The Essential Lenny Bruce.* New York: Panther.

Dagnes, A. (2012). *A Conservative Walks into a Bar: The Politics of Political Humor.* New York: Palgrave Macmillan.

Dani, S. [@sid_dani09]. (2023). @ClareMalone You ruined a man's career and his chance to host the Daily Show. Do you realize that? Your audacity to say, 'We stand by our story,' is appalling. You wrote a hit piece. Journalists like you are causing the public to lose trust and faith in mainstream media. X.

Dauber, J. (2017). *Jewish Comedy: A Serious History.* New York: Norton.

Davis, J. (2015). *Comic Acting and Portraiture in Late-Georgian and Regency England.* Cambridge: Cambridge University Press. https://doi.org/10.1017/CBO9781316162637/.

Dorman, D. (2019). Daphne Dorman (@DaphneDorman). *Twitter.* https://twitter.com/DaphneDorman.

Dorman, D. (29 August 2019). Punching down requires you to consider yourself superior to another group. @DaveChappelle doesn't consider himself better than me in any way. He isn't punching up or punching down. He's punching lines. That's his job and he's a master of his craft. #SticksAndStones #imthatdaphne.

@DaphneDorman. https://twitter.com/DaphneDorman/status/11669377286 81791488.

Double, O. (2014). *Getting the Joke: The Inner Workings of Stand-up Comedy*. London: Bloomsbury Publishing. https://doi.org/10.5040/9781408 177686.

Double, O. (2017). The Origin of the Term Stand-up Comedy. *Comedy Studies*, 8, 106–109. https://doi.org/10.1080/2040610X.2017.1279912.

Downie, J. A. (2005). Public and Private: The Myth of the Bourgeois Public Sphere. In Cynthia Wall, ed., *A Concise Companion to the Restoration and Eighteenth Century*. Malden: Blackwell, 58–79.

Entertainment Tonight. (2022). Will Smith SLAPS Chris Rock at Oscars 2022. www.youtube.com/watch?v=z4t1CC7-UFE.

Elkins, E. (2021). Streaming Diplomacy: Netflix's Domestic Politics and Foreign Policy. In Dal Yong Jin, ed., *The Routledge Handbook of Digital Media and Globalization*. New York: Routledge, 150–57.

Flynn, M. (2019). The U.S. said a California cherry-picker went to Pakistan for terrorist training. Now the case has collapsed. *Washington Post*. www .washingtonpost.com/nation/2019/07/31/us-said-california-cherry-picker-went-pakistan-terrorist-training-now-case-has-collapsed/.

Fraser, N. (1990). Re-thinking the Public Sphere: A Contribution to the Critique of Actually Existing Democracy. *Social Text*, 25(6), 56–80.

Frierson, M. (2020). *Freedom in Laughter: Dick Gregory, Bill Cosby and the Civil Rights Movement*. Albany: SUNY Press.

Foxx, R. and Miller, N. (1977). Dick Gregory, *Redd Foxx Encyclopedia of Black Humor*. Pasadena: W. Ritchie Press.

Gadsby, H. (2022). *Ten Steps to Nanette*. Sydney: Allen & Unwin.

Gadsby, H. (15 December 2023). *Banana Palace*. Arts Centre Melbourne.

Gadsby, H. (2024a). *Hannah Gadsby's Gender Agenda*. Netflix.

Gadsby, H. (13 April 2024b). *Woof!* Arts Centre Melbourne.

Giuffre, L. (2021). From Nanette to Nanettflix – Hannah Gadsby's Challenge to Existing Comedy Convention. *Comedy Studies*, 12 (1), January, 29–39. https://doi.org/10.1080/2040610X.2020.1850102.

Gladstone, B. (2023). The Hasan Minhaj Saga and Evolving Expectations of Truth in Comedy. *On the Media*. www.wnycstudios.org/podcasts/otm/epi sodes/on-the-media-hasan-minhaj-and-evolving-expectations-truth-comedy.

Gold, J. (2020). *Yes, I Can Say That: When They Come for the Comedians, We're All in Trouble*. New York: Dey Street.

Goltz, D. B. (2017). *Comic Performativities: Identity, Internet Outrage, and the Aesthetics of Communication*. New York: Routledge. https://doi.org/10.4324/ 9781315181967.

Goltz, D. B. and Zingsheim, J. (2024). The Performativity of Comedic Apologies. *Text and Performance Quarterly*, 44(1), 15–31. https://doi.org/10.1080/10462937.2023.2168040.

Greenbaum, A. (1999). Stand-up Comedy as Rhetorical Argument: An Investigation of Comic Culture. *Humor – International Journal of Humor Research*, 12(1), 33–46. https://doi.org/10.1515/humr.1999.12.1.33.

Guardian News. (2022). Elon Musk booed by crowd after Dave Chappelle introduces him on stage. www.youtube.com/watch?v=bpfKJo8aYd8.

Haggins, B. (2007). *Laughing Mad: The Black Comic Persona in Post-Soul America*. New Brunswick: Rutgers University Press. https://hdl-handle-net.eu1.proxy.openathens.net/2027/heb08102.0001.001.

Hargrave, M. (2020). Stage Persona, Stand-up Comedy and Mental Health: 'Putting Yourself Out There'. *Persona Studies*, 5, 67–82. https://doi.org/10.21153/psj2019vol5no2art917.

Heim, C. (2016). *Audience as Performer: The Changing Role of Theatre Audiences in the Twenty-First Century*. New York: Routledge.

Herron, S. (2022). *Irony and Earnestness in Eighteenth-Century Literature: Dimensions of Satire and Solemnity*. Cambridge: Cambridge University Press. https://doi.org/10.1017/9781108993227.

Hill, A. (1730). *The Plain Dealer*. London: S. Richardson.

Hobbes, T. (1996). *Hobbes: Leviathan: Revised student edition*. Edited by R. Tuck. Cambridge: Cambridge University Press. https://doi.org/10.1017/CBO9780511808166.

Husband, A. (2018). 'Patriot Act with Hasan Minhaj' Is Already Having an Effect. *Forbes*, www.forbes.com/sites/andrewhusband/2018/11/02/patriot-act-with-hasan-minhaj-saudi-arabia-us-military/.

Jenkins, H. (1992). *What Made Pistachio Nuts?: Early Sound Comedy and the Vaudeville Aesthetic*. New York: Columbia University Press.

Jones, J. (2009). *Entertaining Politics: Satiric Television and Political Engagement*. Mitchellville: Rowman & Littlefield.

Jones, D. (2021). 'The Black Below': Minstrelsy, Satire, and the Threat of Vernacularity. *Theatre Journal*, 73(2), 129–46. https://doi.org/10.1353/tj.2021.0038.

Habermas, J. (1989). *The Structural Transformation of the Public Sphere: An Inquiry into a Category of Bourgeois Society* translated by Thomas Berger. Boston: MIT Press. https://mitpress.mit.edu/9780262581080/the-structural-transformation-of-the-public-sphere/.

Hobbes, M. (2021). Dave Chappelle's 'Some Of My Best Friends Are Trans' Story Doesn't Hold Up. *Confirm My Choices*, https://michaelhobbes.substack.com/p/dave-chappelles-some-of-my-best-friends.

Khalil, J. F. and Zayani, M. (2021). De-Territorialized Digital Capitalism and the Predicament of the Nation-State: Netflix in Arabia. *Media, Culture & Society* 43(2), 201–18. https://doi.org/10.1177/0163443720932505.

Khorana, S. (2022). *Mediated Emotions of Migration: Reclaiming Affect for Agency.* Bristol: Bristol University Press. https://doi.org/10.46692/9781529218251.

Koehn, J. (2022). I Was at Chappelle's Show When Elon Musk Got Booed. Here's What Really Happened. *The San Francisco Standard.* https://sfstandard.com/arts-culture/dave-chappelle-show-elon-musk-booed-chris-rock/.

Kofsky, F. (1974). *Lenny Bruce: The Comedian as Social Critic and Secular Moralist.* New York: Monad Press.

Krefting, R. (2014) *All Joking Aside: American Humor and Its Discontents.* Baltimore: Johns Hopkins. https://www.press.jhu.edu/books/title/10915/all-joking-aside.

Kuipers, G. and Zijp, D. (2024). Humour and the Public Sphere. *The European Journal of Humour Research,* 12(1), 1–14. https://doi.org/10.7592/EJHR.2024.12.1.937.

Lee, S. (2011). *How I Escaped My Certain Fate: The Life and Deaths of a Stand-up Comedian.* London: Faber and Faber.

Lee, S. (2012). *If You Prefer a Milder Comedian, Please Ask for One EP.* London: Faber and Faber.

Lee, B. (2022a). Will Smith Posts Emotional Apology for the Slap: 'I Am Deeply Remorseful'. *The Guardian.* www.theguardian.com/film/2022/jul/29/will-smith-slap-apology-video.

Lee, J. (2022b). *Oriental, Black, and White: The Formation of Racial Habits in American Theater.* Chapel Hill: University of North Carolina Press.

Lee, S. (2022c). Stewart Lee at Harrogate. www.youtube.com/watch?v=-GC7F-2d_xM.

Lejeune, P. (1995). *On Autobiography.* Minneapolis: University of Minnesota Press.

Limbong, A. (2022). Twitter follows Instagram in restricting Ye's account after antisemitic posts. *NPR.* https://www.npr.org/2022/10/09/1127732183/kanye-west-instagram-twitter.

Lloyd, R. (2019). Sarah Silverman Defends Dave Chapelle and Humour that Offends: That's Comedy. *Los Angeles Times.* www.latimes.com/entertainment-arts/tv/story/2019-09-16/emmys-sarah-silverman-i-love-you-america-hulu.

Los Angeles Times [@latimes] (2022). Will Smith slapped Chris Rock at the #Oscars after the comedian made a joke about Jada Pinkett Smith's hair loss while presenting the award for documentary feature. https://latimes.com/entertainment-arts/movies/story/2022-03-27/oscars-2022-will-smith-chris-rock-punch-slap https://t.co/DxKqENRfD3. Twitter.

Malone, C. (2023a). Hasan Minhaj's 'Emotional Truths'. *The New Yorker*. www.newyorker.com/news/annals-of-communications/hasan-minhajs-emotional-truths.

Malone, C. [@ClareMalone]. (2023b). Here's our official statement. I stand by the story and encourage people to read it in full. https://newyorker.com/news/annals-of-communications/hasan-minhajs-emotional-truths https://t.co/QqPzc9njT3. X.

Mandvi, A. (2015). *No Land's Man*. San Francisco: Chronicle Books.

Marshall, P. D. (2014). *Celebrity and Power*. Minneapolis: University of Minnesota Press.

McBeth, M. K., Clemons, R. S. (2011). Is Fake News Real News? The Significance of Stewart and Colbert for Democratic Discourse, Politics, and Policy. In Amarnath Amarasingam, ed., *The Stewart/Colbert Effect: Essays on the Real Impacts of Fake News*. Jefferson: McFarland, 79–98.

McCarthy, T. (2021). Cancel Culture: Dave Chappelle and Other Comedians Who Have Taken Sides. *Fox News*, https://www.foxnews.com/entertainment/dave-chappelle-comedians-cancel-culture.

Mendoza, M. (2022). Elon Musk Gets Booed Onstage as Dave Chappelle Surprises S.F. Crowd. Datebook. *San Francisco Chronicle*. https://datebook.sfchronicle.com/comedy/dave-chappelle-surprises-s-f-crowd-with-elon-musk-during-final-bay-area-tour-stop.

Michael, J. (2018). Religion and Representation in the 'New Brown America' of Muslim Comedy. *Ecumenica*, 11(2), 62–67. https://doi.org/10.5325/ecumenica.11.2.0062.

Minhaj, H. (2023). My Response to the New Yorker article. *YouTube*. www.youtube.com/watch?v=ABiHlt69M-4.

Minhaj, H. and Cunningham, V. (2019). Hasan Minhaj Talks Patriot Act with The New Yorker's Vinson Cunningham. Directed by The 92nd Street Y, New York. *YouTube*, www.youtube.com/watch?v=4RjC1Q-Jli0.

Mintz, L.E. (1996). Humor and Ethnic Stereotypes in Vaudeville and Burlesque. *MELUS*, 21(4), 19–28. https://doi.org/10.2307/467640.

Moon, K. R. (2005). Lee Tung Foo and the Making of a Chinese American Vaudevillian, 1900s–1920s. *Journal of Asian American Studies*, 8(1), 23–48. https://doi.org/10.1353/jaas.2005.0031.

Moraes, L. de (2018). Netflix Launching 'Patriot Act with Hasan Minhaj' in October. *Deadline*. https://deadline.com/2018/08/hasan-minhaj-netflix-patriot-act-debut-october-28-1202443188/.

MrAndocalrisian (2010). Lenny Bruce Standup 1. www.youtube.com/watch?v=-yUTZm5s_G0be.

Nachman, G. (2003). *Seriously Funny: The Rebel Comedians of the 1950s and 1960s*. New York: Pantheon.

Neavitt, M. (2012). Sing Heavenly News: Journalism and Poetic Authority in Samuel Shepheard's *the Faerie King*. *Studies in Philology*, 109, 496–518. www.jstor.org/stable/24392015.

Nesteroff, K. (2023). *Outrageous: A History of Showbiz and the Culture Wars*. New York: Abrams Press.

Ngai, S. (2005). *Ugly Feelings*. Cambridge, MA: Harvard University Press.

O'Neil, C. (2003). Intro – John Edwards. *The Daily Show with Jon Stewart*.

Oppliger, P. A. and Shouse, E. (2020). Introduction: Come to the Dark Side. In P. A. Oppliger and E. Shouse, eds., *The Dark Side of Stand-up Comedy*. London: Palgrave, 3–27. https://doi.org/10.1007/978-3-030-37214-9.

Pennington, R. (2024). *Pop Islam: Seeing American Muslims in Popular Media*. Bloomington: Indiana University Press. https://muse.jhu.edu/pub/3/mono graph/book/120869.

Perrigo, B. (2022). 'The Idea Exposes His Naiveté.' Twitter Employees on Why Elon Musk Is Wrong about Free Speech. *Time*. https://time.com/6167099/ twitter-employees-elon-musk-free-speech/.

Phelan, P. (1993). *Unmarked: The Politics of Performance*. New York: Routledge.

Piccioto, J. (2022). Practising Flow in Marvell and Ashberry. In Matthew C. Augustine, Giulio J. Pertile and Steven N. Zwicker, eds., *Imagining Andrew Marvell at 400*. Oxford: Oxford University Press, 320–41. https:// doi.org/10.5871/bacad/9780197267073.001.0001.

Rancière, J. (2011). *The Emancipated Spectator*. London: Verso.

Rock, C. (2023). *Selective Outrage*. Netflix.

Rourke, C. (1931). *American Humor: A Study of the National Character*. New York: Harcourt, Brace.

Rude, M. (2021). Dave Chappelle Called Hannah Gadsby 'Not Funny' in His Latest Rant. www.out.com/celebs/2021/10/26/dave-chappelle-called-han nah-gadsby-not-funny-his-latest-rant.

Rybarczyk, T. (2004). ACLU says FBI spied on activists, Muslims. *Chicago Tribune*. www.chicagotribune.com/news/ct-xpm-2004-12-03-0412030209-story.html.

Sales, L. (2017). Comedian Hannah Gadsby talks to 7.30 about SSM, abuse and quitting comedy. *ABC News* (Australia). www.youtube.com/watch? v=tbjbTb3s6Xo.

Said, E. (1993). Representation of the Intellectual. *Reith Lectures, BBC*. www .bbc.co.uk/programmes/p00gmx4c.

Schulman, M. (2022). What It Felt Like in the Room When Will Smith Slapped Chris Rock at the Oscars. *The New Yorker*. www.newyorker.com/culture/

culture-desk/what-it-felt-like-in-the-room-when-will-smith-slapped-chris-rock-at-the-oscars.

Sedgman, K. (2017). Audience Experience in an Anti-expert Age: A Survey of Theatre Audience Research. *Theatre Research International*, 42, 307–22. https://doi.org/10.1017/S0307883317000608.

Sennett, R. (1974). *The Fall of Public Man*. London: Penguin Books.

Shouse, E. (2020). Person, Persona, and Act: The Dark and Light Sides of George Carlin, Richard Pryor, and Robin Williams. In A. Oppliger Patrice and Eric Shouse, eds., *The Dark Side of Stand-Up Comedy*, Cham: Springer International, 29–49. https://doi.org/10.1007/978-3-030-37214-9.

Shroff, K. [@KaivanShroff. (2023). @ClareMalone How can you stand by this? Do you dispute any of this? https://t.co/sAkE77l6hw. X.

Silverman, S. (2019). Dave Chapelle Tribute. *Mark Twain Prize at the Kennedey Center*. www.youtube.com/watch?v=B8YnmfjCSgY.

Silverman, S. (2022). Chapelle, B*face, Anything Goes. *The Sarah Silverman Podcast*. www.youtube.com/watch?v=G_ZEKGmXqfw.

Smith, M. and Keane, D. (2019). Hannah Gadsby to use phone-locking technology to stop people filming her shows. *ABC News*. www.abc.net.au/news/2019-03-26/hannah-gadsby-uses-phone-locking-technology-for-latest-tour/10939478.

Sobel, A. (2018). Norm Macdonald Slams 'Nanette,' Defends Roseanne, Louis C. K. *Advocate*. www.advocate.com/arts-entertainment/2018/9/12/norm-macdonald-slams-nanette-defends-roseanne-louis-ck.

Stewart, I. (2019). Netflix Drops Hasan Minhaj Episode in Saudi Arabia at Government's Request. *NPR*. www.npr.org/2019/01/01/681469011/netflix-drops-hasan-minhaj-episode-in-saudi-arabia-at-governments-request.

Tapper, J. (2009). What prompted comedian's tirade against old schoolmate Richard Hammond? *Daily Mail*. www.dailymail.co.uk/tvshowbiz/article-1209921/What-prompted-comedians-tirade-old-schoolmate-Richard-Hammond.html.

Taylor Swift Reacts to Jo Koy's Golden Globes Joke. Directed by Shared News, 2024. *YouTube*, www.youtube.com/watch?v=DfShR35zlTU.

Trilling, L. (1972). *Sincerity and Authenticity*. London: Oxford University Press.

Walsh, S. (2023). 'The Daily Show' Returns to Guest Hosts after Hasan Minhaj Controversy. *Vanity Fair*.

Warner, M. (2002). *Publics and Counterpublics*. Princeton: Princeton University Press.

Wilda, J. (2022). Elon Musk getting booed at Dave Chappelle show Chase Center. www.youtube.com/watch?v=BdBga225HBk.

@willsmith. (2022). Will Smith on Instagram: 'Violence in all of its forms is poisonous and destructive. My behavior at last night's Academy Awards was unacceptable and inexcusable. Jokes at my expense are a part of the job, but a joke about Jada's medical condition was too much for me to bear and I reacted emotionally. I would like to publicly apologize to you, Chris. I was out of line and I was wrong. I am embarrassed and my actions were not indicative of the man I want to be. There is no place for violence in a world of love and kindness. I would also like to apologize to the Academy, the producers of the show, all the attendees and everyone watching around the world. I would like to apologize to the Williams Family and my King Richard Family. I deeply regret that my behavior has stained what has been an otherwise gorgeous journey for all of us. I am a work in progress. Sincerely, Will.' *Instagram*. www.instagram.com/p/CbqmaY1p7Pz/.

Woodhead, C. (21 December 2023). Banana Palace | Hannah Gadsby. *The Age*, www.theage.com.au/culture/live-reviews/cinderella-gets-her-dancing-shoes-on-in-a-show-that-s-perfect-for-children-20231214-p5erh8.html.

Woodroof, Cory. (2024). Taylor Swift's Devastating Look at Jo Koy's Unfunny Golden Globes Joke Became an Instant Meme. *For the Win*, 8 January, https://ftw.usatoday.com/lists/taylor-swifts-devastating-look-at-joe-koys-unfunny-golden-globes-joke-became-an-instant-meme.

Wright, M. (2018). Has Michael Che Seen Nanette? An Investigation. *Vulture*. www.vulture.com/2018/12/has-michael-che-seen-nanette-an-investigation.html.

Zinoman, J. (2023a). Lying in Comedy Isn't Always Wrong, but Hasan Minhaj Crossed a Line. *The New York Times*. www.nytimes.com/2023/09/20/arts/hasan-minhaj-comedy.html.

Zinoman, J. (2023b). Was a Scandal the Best Thing to Happen to Hasan Minhaj? *The New York Times*. www.nytimes.com/2023/12/17/arts/television/hasan-minhaj-the-new-yorker.html.

Acknowledgments

We enjoyed writing this Element and we thank those who supported us to do so: our editor Fintan Walsh; the excellent anonymous reviewers; our colleagues at the University of Melbourne; our comedy comrades Debra Aarons and Til Knowles, who have seen and discussed many shows and ideas with us; our families; and our partners, Marney and Fran.

About the Author

Sarah Balkin's scholarship ranges across nineteenth, twentieth, and twenty-first century literature, theatre, and performance. Her current projects examine the historical emergence of deadpan performance styles (1830-1930) and humourlessness in contemporary queer and feminist comedy. A more detailed survey of her research is available at https://findanexpert.unimelb.edu.au/profile/626364-sarah-balkin.

Marc Mierowsky has published widely on Restoration and eighteenth-century literature. His monograph, A Spy Among Us: Defoe's Secret Service and the Campaign to End Scottish Independence, is forthcoming with Yale University Press. With Debra Aarons he has published on Jewish comedy, licence, obscenity, and comic persona.

About the Series
Contemporary Performance Texts responds to the evolution of the form, role and meaning of text in theatre and performance in the late twentieth and twenty-first centuries, by publishing Elements that explore the generation of text for performance, its uses in performance, and its varied modes of reception and documentation.

Cambridge Elements ≡

Contemporary Performance Texts

Elements in the Series

Printed in the United States
by Baker & Taylor Publisher Services